THE SLOWCOOKER LIBRARY

Convenience Foods for the Slow Cooker

foulsham

The Oriel, Thames Valley Court, 183–187 Bath Road, Slough, Berkshire SL1 4AA, England

Foulsham books can be found in all good bookshops and direct from www.foulsham.com

ISBN: 978-0-572-03532-7

Printed in Great Britain by Printwise (Haverhill) Ltd, Haverhill

THE SLOWCOOKER LIBRARY

Convenience Foods for the Slow Cooker

Carolyn Humphries

foulsham

LONDON • NEW YORK • TORONTO • SYDNEY

contents

introduction

Slow cooking in a crock pot is a wonderful way of ensuring you come home to a sumptuous meal after a busy day. But, quite often, you're expected to do a fair bit of preparation in advance. I don't know about you, but getting up at the crack of dawn to fry-off onions and meat or make an elaborate sauce to pour over the raw ingredients doesn't fill me with enthusiasm. Here is the perfect answer! With all these recipes, there is virtually no work to do beforehand apart from mixing a few things together or, on rare occasions, a small amount of trimming. With a little help from well-chosen convenience foods, for the most part you simply put the ingredients into the pot, switch on and go. Even for some of the dishes that cook more quickly – like fish, for instance – you don't always want to be fiddling around. You just want to pop the ingredients in the cooker, go and have a bath or watch your favourite programme, then dish up. No messing, no fiddling and certainly no special skills required!

Purists will argue that you should be chopping your own onions – in fact, preparing all your vegetables from scratch, making your own pastry (paste) and grating your own cheese. From a financial point of view they are right; it's obviously cheaper to do it that way, but if you balance that against time and effort (and particularly if you don't enjoy doing it), then you can argue it is money well spent.

This has been an eye-opening experience for me. I'm used to preparing everything myself – because I love cooking – but I have been very pleasantly surprised at the quality of the convenience foods I've used and the delicious results I've achieved!

This is the ideal cookbook for non-cooks. Apart from sometimes having to cook some rice, pasta or potatoes, warm some bread or toss a salad before serving, there is little else to be done – and even the effort of doing that can be minimised. With my handy guide to speedy accompaniments on pages 14–19, you'll be able to dish up fabulous, nutritious, perfectly balanced meals while hardly lifting a finger!

using your slow cooker

1 Stand the electric base on a level, heat-resistant surface. Do not use on the floor.

2 Do not preheat your pot unless your manufacturer's instructions tell you to.

3 Put the ingredients in the ceramic crock pot, then put the pot in the base.

4 Cover with the lid and select the cooking temperature – High, Medium (if you have it) or Low. Note that some smaller cookers cook quite quickly on High, so you may find that cooking on the Low setting is preferable, particularly if you are not going to be there to keep an eye on things or are cooking only a smallish quantity.

5 Cook for the recommended time. If there is a range of time, check after the shorter time given; this will usually be sufficient for most cookers but the food won't spoil if it is cooked for the extra time, particularly if cooked on Low.

6 Taste, stir and re-season, if necessary.

7 Switch off the cooker and remove the crock pot using oven gloves.

cooking tips for the slow cooker

- Any of your usual soup, stew or casserole recipes can be cooked in your slow cooker. However, liquid doesn't evaporate as much as it does when cooking conventionally, so cut down the liquid content by 30–50 per cent (not necessary for soups) or increase the flour or cornflour (cornstarch) thickener by a third. You can always add a little extra liquid at the end.

- Use a crock pot suitable for the quantity of food you want to cook. It should be at least ⅓–½ full for the best results (but for foods like ribs or chicken wings, a single layer is fine if you have a large pot). Don't use a small pot and pack the food in tightly to the top or the heat won't be able to penetrate the food – just as when cooking conventionally. But, conversely, don't have too little either. For instance, one chop in the pot will overcook unless the pot is filled up to at least a third with liquid. So, if cooking for one, you may need to double the amount of liquid to be on the safe side.

- When cooking meat and root vegetables together, put the vegetables towards the bottom of the pot as they will take longer to cook than the meat.

- Do not cook too large a joint or bird in the crock pot. It should fit in the pot with at least a 2.5 cm/1 in headspace. If unsure, cut the joint or bird in half before cooking. (It will then cook quicker, as when cooking conventionally.)

- When cooking soups, make sure there is a 5 cm/2 in headspace in the pot to allow for bubbling during cooking.

- Most foods can be cooked on High or Low (or Medium or Auto-cook if you have it). Fish, rice and egg-based dishes, however, are best cooked on Low.

- If you are planning to be out all day, opt for cooking on Low, then there is little or no chance of the meal ruining even if you are late (particularly if you don't have a programmable slow cooker).

- Do not open the lid unnecessarily during cooking as heat will be lost. If you remove it to add extra ingredients or to stir more than once or twice, you may need to add an extra 10 minutes at the end (but in most cases there is sufficient cooking time allowed in the recipes for this).

- Should there be too much liquid at the end of cooking, strain it into a saucepan and boil rapidly for several minutes until reduced to the quantity and consistency you require, or thicken it with a little flour or cornflour (cornstarch) blended to a smooth paste with a little water and cook for 1 minute, stirring.

- When food is cooked, the cooker can be switched off and left for up to 30 minutes. The food will be still piping hot. If you need to keep food hot for longer, switch to Low. (This isn't suitable for egg-based or rice dishes.)

- If you are unsure whether a joint of meat or a bird is cooked through, insert a meat thermometer into the thickest part of the joint at the end of cooking. The temperature should reach a minimum of 63°C/145°F for rare beef to a maximum of 71°C/165°F for chicken.

- You can use the crock pot to keep hot drinks (such as mulled wine) warm, or for hot dips or fondues. Keep the pot on the Low setting.

- Frozen vegetables and fish can be cooked from frozen.

looking after your slow cooker

- Do not put the crock pot or the lid in the oven, freezer or microwave, on the hob or under the grill (broiler).

- Do not plunge the hot pot into cold water after cooking because it may crack.

- Do not leave the whole pot soaking in water as the base is unglazed and porous so will absorb the water. You may, however, leave water in the pot to soak it before washing.

- Do not preheat the cooker before adding the ingredients (unless your manufacturer's instructions tell you to).

- Do not use the slow cooker to reheat food.

- Do not leave uncooked food in the slow cooker when it is not switched on, so never put it in there overnight ready to switch on in the morning. Store the ingredients in the fridge.

- Do not use abrasive cleaners on the crock pot – but it will be dishwasher safe.

- Do not immerse the electric base in water; simply unplug it and wipe it clean with a damp cloth.

cooking times

Some crock pots now have three settings, but others have only two. I have cooked most foods on High or Low as they will be relevant to all. Use Medium or Low for any of them, if you prefer, and adjust the times according to the chart below. However, please remember that when cooking fish, rice and eggs you will almost always need to use Low.

Some cookers also have Auto-cook; follow your manufacturer's guidelines to use it. I recommend you use Low if you are going to be out all day.

This chart also shows you the approximate conversion times for conventionally cooked soups, stews and casseroles, should you want to try your own recipes (but remember to reduce the liquid by at least a third). Always check your manufacturer's instructions, too, as the times may vary slightly.

The more you cook, the more used to the correct times for your cooker you'll become!

Most slow-cooking books recommend you add boiling liquid to the ingredients. In this book, in many cases, all the ingredients are cold, in which case the cooking time is increased by about 1 hour on High or 2 hours on Low.

Please note that the cooking time will be longer for the recipes that don't have boiling liquid added.

Conventional cooking time	Slow cooking time in hours		
	High	Medium	Low
15–30 minutes	1–2	2–3	4–6
30 minutes–1 hour	2–3	3–4	5–7
1–2 hours	3–4	4–6	6–8
2–4 hours	5–6	6–8	8–12

speedy accompaniments

Since it's the flavour and imagination of a good meal you are interested in, not spending ages in the kitchen, you are hardly likely to want to waste time preparing the bits and pieces to go with your main meal. No problem! Here are some quick ideas for how to do the last-minute side dishes quickly and easily.

Rice

For many people, cooking rice can be a disaster; you end up with a stodgy, gloopy mess. For those of you who fall into that category, buy boil-in-the-bag or microwave rice. You can choose from all sorts of varieties to suit the meal. They may be slightly more expensive than the plain old grains, but if you follow the manufacturer's instructions, you'll get great results.

For those of you who want to try, though, here are my top tips for cooking from scratch:

- Wash the rice first to remove excess starch.

- Always use a large pan with plenty of water, with a pinch of salt added, if liked.

- Add the rice only when the water is boiling rapidly.

- Stir once. Do not cover the pan.

- Cook for the time it says on the packet (for most long-grain varieties it's 10 minutes).

- Just before the time is up, taste a grain or two. There should be just a little resistance to your teeth. Do not overcook.

- Drain the rice in a fine colander or a sieve (strainer), rinse with boiling water to separate the grains and drain again.

- Place the colander over the pan with a little water in it over a gentle heat, to dry out briefly.

Pasta

Dried pasta is relatively easy to cook (see below) but for quickness – and quality – use fresh pasta, which takes only a few minutes in boiling water. Alternatively, use dried Chinese egg or rice noodles, which just need standing in boiling water for 5 minutes and then draining, or fresh ones, which can be added directly to the meal in the crock pot for a few minutes to heat through.

Top tips for cooking from scratch:

- Always use a large pan with plenty of water, with a pinch of salt added, if liked.

- Add the pasta only when the water is boiling rapidly.

- Stir. Do not cover the pan.

- Cook for the time it says on the packet

- Just before the time is up, take out a piece and taste it. There should be just a little resistance to your teeth. Do not overcook.

- Drain the pasta in a colander. No need to rinse (unlike rice) as you want the sauce to adhere to the pasta.

Other grains

Couscous and bulghar (cracked wheat) are great accompaniments and almost foolproof to prepare.

- Use one part grain to two parts boiling water or stock.

- Stir the grains into the measured boiling liquid, with a pinch of salt added, if liked.

- Stir, cover and leave to stand. Allow 5 minutes for couscous and 15 minutes for bulghar.

- Fluff up with a fork and serve.

Potatoes

I don't recommend using frozen or the instant varieties as accompaniments. Canned are not that palatable as they are, either, but can be good sautéed. Drain them and then dry them thoroughly with kitchen paper (paper towels), then sauté in a little hot oil or in oil and butter, shaking the pan or turning them occasionally until golden. Sometimes they spit a bit, so I recommend using a covered pan or a splatter guard.

For quickness using fresh, buy pre-washed potatoes, but I recommend you rinse them under the tap before use. No need to peel or scrape. The skin is really good for you.

To microwave
- For jacket potatoes or mash, allow a large-ish pre-washed potato per person. Prick all over with a fork and microwave on High for 3–4 minutes per potato until soft when squeezed.

- For jacket potatoes: serve as they are or pop under a preheated grill (broiler) for a couple of minutes, turning once to crisp the skins.

- For mash: when cooked, put in a bowl and crush with a potato masher, adding a knob of butter, a dash of milk and some seasoning. No need to peel; the skin is good for you and adds texture. It's very trendy to serve crushed potatoes rather than creamy mash. They are simply roughly crushed with a little butter and seasoning – even less work!

To boil

- For jacket potatoes: prick the skins of large potatoes and boil in water until just tender. Drain, pat dry on kitchen paper (paper towels), then grill (broil) as above to crisp the skins.

- For boiled potatoes: boil small, even-sized washed potatoes in water, with a pinch of salt, if liked, until just tender. Drain.

To roast

- I have tried the frozen roast potatoes and they do come out lovely and golden and crispy, but the calorie and fat content is huge! For a more nutritious but equally quick alternative that's different but just as delicious, toss small washed potatoes in a little olive or sunflower oil (just one or two tablespoonfuls depending on the quantity of potatoes) in a roasting tin, sprinkle with salt (and scatter in some sesame or caraway seeds, if liked). Roast in a preheated oven at 230°C/450°F/gas 8/fan oven 210°C for about 30 minutes until golden and tender, turning and rearranging once, if possible.

Oven wedges

- Use frozen or cut some washed potatoes into 6–8 wedges. Put in a roasting tin with 15–30 ml/1–2 tbsp of olive or sunflower oil and add a pinch of salt or 15 ml/1 tbsp of Cajun seasoning. Toss, then bake at 220°C/425°F/gas 7/fan oven 200°C for about 25 minutes, turning and rearranging once, if possible, until golden and soft.

Salads

No-fuss green salad
- Obviously, buying pre-prepared leaves is the quickest. Use bought dressing of your choice or try drizzling with just a little olive oil, a splash of balsamic condiment, a good grinding of black pepper and a pinch of dried oregano.

Easy tomato salad
- Use cherry tomatoes, simply cut into halves. Toss with a little olive oil and white balsamic condiment, a good grinding of black pepper and some torn fresh basil leaves. If you haven't any fresh herbs, add a good sprinkling of dried chives.

Convenience salads

Mixed salad
- You can buy ready-prepared mixed salads, but they don't keep and are very expensive, so I would argue that it's best to buy the ready-prepared leaves or tear up your own from a lettuce head. Throw in some whole or halved cherry tomatoes, and dice some cucumber. If you want onion rings in your salad, take a whole onion, don't peel it, just cut it into round slices, then separate into rings, discarding the outer two layers. Easy! You could add drained, canned sweetcorn, whole or sliced radishes and/or thawed frozen or fresh shelled peas.

Chinese salad
- Just mix 30–45 ml/2–3 tbsp of sunflower oil with a tablespoonful of soy sauce and a squeeze of lemon juice. If you like it a bit sweeter, add 5 ml/1 tsp of clear honey, too, then add a packet of fresh, ready-prepared shredded stir-fry vegetables, toss and serve.

Bean salad

- Try drained canned beans and sweetcorn, or green beans, mixed with a little thawed frozen chopped onion or chopped garlic from a jar, a pinch of salt, a good grinding of black pepper, a drizzle of olive oil and a splash of white balsamic condiment (or wine vinegar and 5 ml/1 tsp of caster (superfine) sugar).

Russian salad

- Use a well-drained can of mixed vegetables and mix with mayonnaise and a good grinding of black pepper – a classic!

Rice or pasta salad

- Mix leftover cooked rice or pasta shapes with some canned pineapple, thawed sliced frozen peppers, thawed frozen peas, a little diced onion and a pinch of crushed dried chilli flakes. Moisten it all with a little mayonnaise and a splash of the pineapple juice.

notes on the recipes

- Most of these recipes are best cooked in a large, oval 6.5 litre/ 11½ pint slow cooker but the majority can be cooked in a smaller, round 3.5 litre/6 pint cooker. Remember that some small models cook quite quickly on High, so you may prefer the Low setting.

- All ingredients are given in imperial, metric and American measures. Follow one set only. American terms are given in brackets.

- The ingredients are listed in the order in which they are used.

- All spoon measures are level: 1 tsp=5 ml; 1 tbsp=15 ml.

- Eggs are medium unless otherwise stated.

- Where I've called for dried onion flakes, it's because chopped raw onion, without pre-frying, has too strong a flavour for that particular dish. However, in rich sauces I've sometimes used frozen chopped, mixed with a little oil or softened butter, which seems to take away the pungency. For strong-flavoured food, raw on its own is fine.

- Seasoning is very much a matter of personal taste. Taste the food before serving and adjust to suit your own palate.

- Fresh herbs are great for garnishing and adding flavour. Pots of them are available in all good supermarkets. Keep your favourite ones on the windowsill and water regularly. Jars of ready-prepared herbs and frozen ones – chopped parsley and coriander (cilantro) in particular – are also very useful.

- TOP TIP: Pop a pack of fresh parsley or coriander in the freezer. When hard crush it whilst still in the bag instead of chopping, then tip the crushed leaves into a sealable container and store in the freezer to use as required.

- When I call for stock, obviously, fresh is best, but for quickness, I recommend a good quality stock concentrate in a bottle. You can also use cubes or powder if you prefer, made up according to the manufacturer's directions.

- All can and packet sizes are approximate as they vary from brand to brand.

- I recommend you choose free-range, outdoor-reared meat and poultry or look for the RSPCA Monitored Freedom Food label and avoid intensively reared produce. When buying cured meats and sausages, make sure they are at least, labelled 'farm assured', which offers some guarantees of acceptable animal welfare.

- If you haven't time to weigh your frozen vegetables, as a guide:

  For chunky ones, such as broccoli florets, 2 large handfuls = about 225 g/8 oz

  For small ones, such as sliced mushrooms, 2 large handfuls = about 100 g/4 oz.

soups

Soups are standard fare for the slow cooker and a great way of getting the family to eat vegetables.

So that you don't have to be bothered with loads of chopping, I've used mostly frozen vegetables, which are as nutritious as fresh. But look out, too, for ready-prepared fresh ones that are reduced for quick sale. If you can't use them that day, pop them, still sealed in their bag or container, in the freezer for up to a week. Because you're going to slow cook them, it won't matter that they will go a bit limp on thawing. However, the ones frozen at source will have a higher nutritional value than the cut-up fresh ones that have been sitting in the chiller cabinet of the supermarket for several days, as they begin to lose nutrients as soon as they are peeled, chopped or shredded.

Tips for great slow-cooked soups

- Allow a 5 cm/2 in headspace in the pot when you are cooking soups to allow for bubbling during cooking.

- If the finished soup is too thick, you can always thin it down with a little boiling water or stock.

- If the finished result is too thin, remove the lid and cook on High for 15 minutes to thicken the soup.

- For extra richness, stir in a spoonful of cream to thick soups just before serving.

- Add a splash of wine or brandy to a hearty soup to add depth.

- Taste and your soups and adjust the seasoning to taste. A dash of Worcestershire sauce at the end of cooking will perk up a plain soup.

- Most ordinary soup recipes can be used in the slow cooker. There's generally less evaporation, so you can reduce the liquid content by 30 per cent if you like a thicker soup.

- You can make a meal of most soup recipes by serving with your favourite crusty bread, pittas or rolled tortillas.

cauliflower & broccoli soup

4-6

2 hrs HIGH or 4 hrs LOW

Crusty bread

Chef's note

This is a delicious creamy, almost velvety soup with a rich flavour. You can, of course, use a small head of broccoli and half a small cauliflower, cut into florets (or just a whole small cauliflower and omit the broccoli) in place of the frozen, if you prefer.

450 g/1 lb **fresh or frozen broccoli and cauliflower florets**

8 washed **baby potatoes**

30 ml/2 tbsp **dried onion flakes**

900 ml/1½ pts/3¾ cups boiling **vegetable stock**

1 **bouquet garni sachet**

Salt and freshly ground black pepper

100 g/4 oz/1 cup grated strong **Cheddar cheese**

60 ml/4 tbsp **dried milk powder** (non-fat dry milk)

A little chopped fresh or frozen **parsley** to garnish

1   Put the broccoli and cauliflower, potatoes, onion flakes, stock and bouquet garni in the crock pot. Season well.

2   Cover and cook on High for 2 hours or Low for 4 hours until the vegetables are really tender.

3   Discard the bouquet garni, then tip the soup into a blender or food processor, add the cheese and milk powder and run the machine until smooth.

4   Pour the mixture back into the crock pot, cover and leave on Low to heat through for 5 minutes or until ready to serve.

5   Taste and re-season, if necessary. Ladle into warm bowls and garnish with parsley.

6   Serve with crusty bread.

Serving tip
• This is quite filling, so don't serve it as a starter unless you are really hungry!

brussels soup with nutmeg

4-6

3 hrs HIGH or **6** hrs LOW

Fresh white bread

450 g/1 lb fresh or **frozen Brussels sprouts**

4 washed small **potatoes**

45 ml/3 tbsp **plain (all-purpose) flour**

30 ml/2 tbsp **dried onion flakes**

1 **bouquet garni sachet**

900 ml/1½ pts/3¾ cups boiling **chicken or vegetable stock**

Salt and freshly ground black pepper

A good pinch of **ground nutmeg**

120 ml/4 fl oz/½ cup **single (light) cream**

1   Put the sprouts in the crock pot with the potatoes, add the flour and toss so everything is coated in the flour. Add the onion flakes and bouquet garni, then pour on the boiling stock. Stir well and season with salt, pepper and the nutmeg.

2   Cover and cook on High for 3 hours or Low for 6 hours until the sprouts and potatoes are really tender.

3   Discard the bouquet garni, then tip the soup into a blender or food processor and add all but 30 ml/2 tbsp of the cream. Run the machine until smooth.

4   Taste and re-season, if necessary, then return to the crock pot on Low until ready to serve.

5   Ladle the soup into bowls and garnish with a swirl of the remaining cream.

6   Serve with fresh white bread.

Freezing tip
• If you enjoy soup, why not make extra and freeze some handy-sized portions?

chilli beef potage

Chef's note

Hearty and warming, this soup is perfect for a winter lunch or supper. Try serving it with a packet of ready-made croûtons or some crushed plain corn tortilla chips to throw in at the table, some flour tortillas rolled up – or even just fresh crusty bread!

4

2 hrs HIGH
or **4** hrs LOW

Croûtons or
tortilla chips

225 g/8 oz/2 cups **free-flow frozen minced (ground) beef**

5 ml/1 tsp chopped **garlic** from a jar, or 1 **garlic clove**, chopped

2.5 ml/½ tsp **ground cumin**

1.5–2.5 ml/¼–½ tsp **crushed dried chillies**, or to taste

A good handful of **frozen sliced mixed (bell) peppers**, or 1 large fresh **pepper**, sliced

400 g/14 oz/1 large can of **red kidney beans**, drained

900 ml/1½ pts/3¾ cups boiling **beef stock**

30 ml/2 tbsp **tomato purée** (paste)

2.5 ml/½ tsp **dried oregano**

A good pinch of **caster (superfine) sugar**

Salt and freshly ground black pepper

20 ml/4 tsp **soured (dairy sour) cream** to garnish (optional)

1 Spread out the minced beef evenly in the crock pot. Add all the remaining ingredients except the soured cream garnish, if using, and stir well.

2 Cover and cook on High for 2 hours or Low for 4 hours until everything is tender.

3 Taste and re-season if necessary. Ladle into warm bowls and garnish each with a little soured cream, if liked.

4 Serve with croûtons or tortilla chips.

Cook's tip

• It's important to use free-flow frozen mince so the grains of meat remain separate.

chicken noodle soup

4

3 hrs HIGH
or **6** hrs LOW

Pitta bread

Chef's note

This soup has plenty of chicken and noodles to make it really tasty and is a far cry from the watery versions you may have tasted in the past. It couldn't be simpler to make so you'll soon find it's a family favourite.

3 skinless **chicken thighs**

1 **onion**, washed and halved (no need to peel, just discard any loose outer layers)

1 **bay leaf**

1 slab of dried medium **egg noodles**, crumbled

900 ml/1½ pts/3¾ cups boiling **chicken stock**

Salt and freshly ground black pepper

A little chopped fresh or frozen **parsley** to garnish

1. Put all the ingredients except the parsley garnish in the crock pot.

2. Cover and cook on High for 3 hours or Low for 6 hours.

3. Discard the bay leaf. Lift the chicken out of the pot with a draining spoon. Pull all the meat off the bones, using a knife and fork, and cut into small pieces.

4. Return the meat to the crock pot, taste and re-season if necessary. Ladle into warm bowls and sprinkle with chopped parsley.

5. Serve with pitta bread.

Serving tip

- If you want to transform this into a more substantial lunch or supper dish, fill the pitta bread with your favourite salad ingredients and a little mayonnaise or other favourite dressing.

butternut squash soup

4-6

3 hrs HIGH
or **6** hrs LOW

Crusty bread

Chef's note

Golden, warming, soothing, delicious – that's four adjectives that perfectly describe this easy-to-make soup. You can, of course, prepare your own squash (or use pumpkin instead) but this is the fast way.

15 ml/1 tbsp softened **butter**

A good handful of **frozen diced onion**, or 1 large **fresh onion**, chopped

500 g/1¼ lb frozen or fresh diced **butternut squash**

4 washed small **potatoes**

2.5 ml/½ tsp **ground cumin**

2.5 ml/½ tsp **paprika**

2.5 ml/½ tsp **dried mixed herbs**

5 ml/1 tsp **caster (superfine) sugar**

900 ml /1½ pints/3¾ cups boiling **chicken or vegetable stock**

Salt and freshly ground black pepper

15 ml/1 tbsp **single (light) cream**

1   Mix the butter with the onion in the crock pot, then add all the remaining ingredients except the cream.

2   Cover and cook on High for 3 hours or Low for 6 hours until the squash and potatoes are very tender.

3   When the soup is cooked, tip into a blender or food processor and run the machine until it is a smooth purée. Taste and re-season if necessary.

4   Return the soup to the crock pot on Low to keep warm until ready to serve ladled into warm soup bowls.

5   Swirl the cream into the soup and serve with crusty bread.

Serving tip
• For an even richer result, try a spoonful of mascarpone in the soup.

chicken, corn & shiitake soup

Chef's note

Normally when you use dried mushrooms you need to reconstitute them first, but here the long, slow cooking plumps them up beautifully and they impart a delicious, intense flavour.

6

4 hrs HIGH
or **8** hrs LOW

Prawn crackers

A good handful of **frozen diced onion**, or 1 **fresh onion**, chopped

225 g/8 oz/2 cups **frozen sweetcorn**

60 ml/4 tbsp **dried shiitake mushrooms**

10 ml/2 tsp **root ginger** from a jar, or use freshly grated

5 ml/1 tsp **chopped garlic** from a jar, or 1 **garlic clove**, chopped

10 ml/2 tsp **dried chives**

2 skinless **chicken thighs**

900 ml/1½ pts/3¾ cups boiling **chicken stock**

45 ml/3 tbsp **cornflour** (cornstarch)

30 ml/2 tbsp **dry sherry**

30 ml/2 tbsp **soy sauce**

1 Put all the ingredients except the cornflour, sherry and soy sauce in the crock pot.

2 Blend the cornflour with the sherry and soy sauce and stir in.

3 Cover and cook on High for 3–4 hours or Low for 6–8 hours until the mushrooms are tender.

4 Lift the chicken out of the pot with a draining spoon. Pull off the meat with a knife and fork and cut in small pieces. Return to the soup.

5 Ladle into warm bowls.

6 Serve with prawn crackers.

Cook's tip

• If you can't find dried shiitake mushrooms, use mixed dried mushrooms instead.

vegetable & tomato soup

4

3 hrs HIGH
or **6** hrs LOW

Hot buttered toast

Chef's note

When I created this soup I was amazed that it was reminiscent of a famous canned variety! Choose the original kind of mixed vegetables with tiny carrots, peas, sweetcorn and beans – you don't want any large chunks.

350 g/12 oz **frozen diced mixed vegetables**

30 ml/2 tbsp **dried onion flakes**

60 ml/4 tbsp **cornflour** (cornstarch)

60 ml/4 tbsp **tomato purée** (paste)

900 ml/1½ pts/3¾ cups boiling **chicken or vegetable stock**

5 ml/1 tsp **dried mixed herbs**

10 ml/2 tsp **caster (superfine) sugar**

Salt and freshly ground black pepper

1   Put the vegetables and onion flakes in the crock pot and stir in the cornflour. Stir in the tomato purée and stock and add the herbs, sugar and a little salt and pepper.

2   Cover and cook on High for 3 hours or Low for 6 hours until really tender and slightly thickened.

3   Taste and re-season, if necessary. Ladle into warm bowls and serve with hot buttered toast.

Serving tip
• Try it topped with grated cheese or some crisp, crumbled bacon.

spinach & broad bean soup

2 hrs HIGH
or 4 hrs LOW

Crusty bread rolls

30 ml/2 tbsp **dried onion flakes**

4 washed small **potatoes** or 1 large **potato**, diced

350 g/12 oz ready-washed fresh or frozen **spinach**

225 g/8 oz **frozen broad (fava) beans**

2.5 ml/½ tsp **dried mixed herbs**

Salt and freshly ground black pepper

A good pinch of **ground nutmeg**

900 ml/1½ pts/3¾ cups boiling **chicken or vegetable stock**

120 ml/4 fl oz/½ cup **single (light) cream**

4 **eggs**

30 ml/2 tbsp **lemon juice**

4 small sprigs of **parsley** to garnish (optional)

1   Put all the ingredients except the cream, eggs, lemon juice and parsley garnish in the crock pot, seasoning to taste with salt and pepper.

2   Cover and cook on High for 2 hours or Low for 4 hours until everything is tender.

3   When the soup is cooked, tip into a blender or food processor, add the cream and run the machine until it is a smooth purée. Taste and re-season with more nutmeg, salt and pepper, if necessary.

4   Return to the crock pot on Low.

5   When ready to serve, poach the eggs in water with the lemon juice added (or use an egg poacher) for 3 minutes or until cooked to your liking.

6   Quickly ladle the soup into warm shallow bowls. Using a draining spoon, if cooked in water and lemon juice, lift out the eggs one at a time and slide one into each bowl. If using a poacher, loosen the eggs and gently tip them into the soup so they slide out of the cups yolk-side up. Garnish each with a small sprig of parsley and serve with crusty bread rolls.

Cook's tip

• Parsley is easy to grow in a pot on the windowsill and you can use it to flavour and garnish so many dishes.

red lentil & carrot soup

Chef's note

Thick, rich and warming, this delicious soup is a real rib-sticker, perfect to greet you when you come home from work on a dark, winter evening. It makes a substantial lunch or supper with lots of crusty bread.

 **4**

 **3** hrs HIGH or **6** hrs LOW

 Crusty bread

100 g/4 oz/⅔ cup **red lentils**

30 ml/2 tbsp **dried onion flakes**

400 g/14 oz/large can of **tomatoes**

225 g/8 oz **frozen carrots**

4 washed small **potatoes**

A good pinch of **caster (superfine) sugar**

15 ml/1 tbsp **tomato purée (paste)**

5 ml/1 tsp **ground cumin**

10 ml/2 tsp chopped fresh or frozen **coriander** (cilantro)

Salt and freshly ground black pepper

900 ml/1½ pts pt/3¾ cups boiling **chicken or vegetable stock**

20 ml/4 tsp **plain yoghurt** and a little **paprika** to garnish

1 Put all the ingredients except the yoghurt and paprika garnish in the crock pot.

2 Cover and cook on High for 3 hours or Low for 6 hours until everything is really soft.

3 When the soup is cooked, tip into a blender or food processor and run the machine until it is a smooth purée. Taste and re-season, if necessary.

4 Return to the crock pot, cover and leave on Low until ready to serve.

5 Ladle into warm bowls and garnish each with a swirl of yoghurt and a sprinkling of paprika.

6 Serve with crusty bread.

Serving tip

• If you don't like your soup quite so thick, after puréeing add some extra stock or some milk to thin it to the consistency you prefer.

tomato, bean & basil soup

Chef's note

This soup can be cooked in a saucepan, of course, but this way you can leave it on Low – even much longer than I have said here. It won't spoil; the flavour will just get better and better!

6

2 hrs HIGH or 4 hrs LOW

Ciabatta bread

2 thick slices of **ciabatta** or other white bread

400 g/14 oz/large can of **haricot (navy) beans**, drained

2 x 400 g/14 oz/large cans of **chopped tomatoes**

30 ml/2 tbsp **dried onion flakes**

5 ml/1 tsp **chopped garlic** from a jar, or 1 **garlic clove**, chopped

10 ml/2 tsp **caster (superfine) sugar**

15 ml/1 tbsp **tomato purée** (paste)

15 ml/1 tbsp **white balsamic condiment**

45 ml/3 tbsp **olive oil**

300 ml/½ pt/1¼ cups boiling **chicken or vegetable stock**

Salt and freshly ground black pepper

30 ml/2 tbsp chopped **fresh basil**

6 tiny sprigs of **basil** to garnish

1   Soak the bread in water for 2 minutes, then squeeze out the excess water and crumble the bread into the crock pot. Add the beans, tomatoes, onion flakes, garlic, sugar, tomato purée, balsamic condiment, oil, stock and salt and pepper.

2   Cover and cook on High for 2 hours or Low for 4 hours until everything is really soft and pulpy.

3   Stir the soup thoroughly, then stir in the chopped basil. Taste and re-season, if necessary.

4   Ladle into warm bowls and garnish each serving with a tiny sprig of basil. Serve with ciabatta bread.

Serving tip

• This doesn't really need an accompaniment, but you could indulge yourself with some garlic bread if you are really hungry.

lamb, barley & vegetable soup

4

4 hrs HIGH or **8** hrs LOW

Crusty bread

Chef's note

I've used a meaty lamb bone left over from the Sunday roast, but you could also use two or three scrag end (stewing lamb) pieces or one lamb shank (but they're quite expensive). It makes a really hearty meal for lunch or supper with some crusty bread.

85 g/3½ oz/½ cup **pearl barley**

1 meaty **roasted shoulder or leg of lamb bone**

A good handful of **frozen diced onion**, or 1 **fresh onion**, chopped

225 g/8 oz **frozen diced mixed vegetables**

900 ml/1½ pts/3¾ cups boiling **lamb or chicken stock**

1 **bay leaf**

Salt and freshly ground black pepper

30 ml/2 tbsp chopped fresh or frozen **parsley**

1   Put all the ingredients except the parsley in the crock pot.

2   Cover and cook on High for 4 hours or Low for 8 hours.

3   Lift the lamb out of the pot and cut all the bits of meat off the
    bone. Cut into small pieces and return to the pot.

4   Discard the bay leaf, taste and re-season, if necessary, then
    stir in the parsley.

5   Ladle into warm bowls.

6   Serve with crusty bread

Serving tip
• You could follow this with some cheese and fruit for a complete meal.

chicken & poultry dishes

As you won't be bothering to pre-brown your meat for the recipes in this book, I often call for skinned pieces, which don't need to look brown to be appetising. It's also better for your health not to eat the skin. All types of birds keep beautifully moist when slow cooked, and as they are so versatile, you can create dishes from all over the world. I've used canned and frozen vegetables for their convenience factor, but you can, of course, always buy ready prepared fresh (though these are not as healthy as frozen as they lose nutrients as soon as they are cut and exposed to the air) or do your own peeling and chopping and add those instead (which will be cheaper).

Tips for great slow-cooked chicken

- It is best to remove skin from poultry before slow cooking.

- Only cook a whole bird if it fits in the crock pot with at least a 2.5 cm/1 in headspace. If you are unsure, cut the joint or bird in half before cooking. (It will then cook quicker, as when cooking conventionally.)

- Defrost frozen chicken thoroughly before cooking.

- If you are unsure whether a joint of meat or a bird is cooked through, insert a meat thermometer into the thickest part of the joint at the end of cooking – the temperature should reach 71°C/165°F – or pierce the thickest part of the joint with a skewer and make sure the juices run clear.

- Smaller portions will obviously cook more quickly, so if you adapt ingredients, keep an eye on the cooking time to make sure the dish does not overcook.

- Place chicken on top of vegetables if you are cooking them together.

- A spoonful of tomato purée (paste) adds colour and flavour to chicken dishes.

- Reduce the liquid by about one-third when you adapt conventional recipes.

red pepper chicken

4

3 hrs HIGH or **6** hrs LOW

Ribbon noodles and a green salad

30 ml/2 tbsp **cornflour** (cornstarch)

Salt and freshly ground black pepper

4 skinless **chicken breasts**

2 good handfuls of **frozen sliced mixed (bell) peppers**, or 1 red and 1 green **pepper**, sliced

65 g/2½ oz **ready-sliced pepperoni**

400 g/14 oz/1 large can of **chopped tomatoes**

60 ml/4 tbsp **dry white wine**

15 ml/1 tbsp **tomato purée** (paste)

5 ml/1 tsp **caster (superfine) sugar**

1.5 ml/¼ tsp **crushed dried chillies** or **chopped chillies** from a jar

5 ml/1 tsp **chopped garlic** from a jar, or 1 **garlic clove**, chopped

2.5 ml/½ tsp **dried oregano**

2.5 ml/½ tsp **pimentón** (smoked paprika)

1   Mix the cornflour with a little salt and pepper in the crock pot. Add the chicken and turn to coat completely. Add all the remaining ingredients and stir well.

2   Cover and cook on High for 3 hours or Low for 6 hours until the chicken is really tender.

3   Taste and re-season if necessary.

4   Serve spooned over ribbon noodles with a crisp green salad.

Cook's tip
• Use ready diced or the small, thickly sliced pieces of chorizo instead of pepperoni, if you prefer.

slow-roast stuffed chicken

4

3 hrs HIGH
or **6** hrs LOW

Your usual
vegetable
accompaniments

Chef's note

Roasting a bird by the slow cooking method keeps it moist and also saves on fuel. In this recipe I suggest popping it in a very hot oven for 30 minutes at the end to firm up the flesh and to crisp and brown the skin at the same time as you cook some roast potatoes (see page 17). But you don't have to do that; just cook it for the longer time, then let it rest while you thicken the gravy.

85 g/3½ oz packet of **sage and onion or sausage and thyme stuffing mix**

A handful of **raisins**

Sunflower oil for greasing

1 oven-ready **chicken**, about 1.5 kg/3 lb

5 ml/1 tsp **soy sauce**

300 ml/½ pt/1¼ cups boiling **chicken stock**

45 ml/3 tbsp **plain (all-purpose) flour**

45 ml/3 tbsp **water**

Salt and freshly ground black pepper

1   Make up the stuffing mix with boiling water according to the packet directions and stir in the raisins. Use some to stuff the neck end of the bird and secure the flap of skin with a skewer. Put the remaining stuffing on a piece of greased foil and fold up to form a parcel.

2   Place a double thickness of foil in the crock pot so it comes up the sides of the pot (to enable easy removal of the bird after cooking). Brush the foil with oil.

3   Place the bird on the foil in the crock pot and brush with the soy sauce. Rest the foil packet of stuffing at the leg end. Pour the boiling stock around.

4   Cover and cook on High for 2–3 hours or Low for 4–6 hours until the bird is cooked through and the juices run clear when pierced with a skewer in the thickest part of the leg.

5   Using the foil, lift the bird out of the pot and transfer it to a roasting tin (still on the foil). Roast in a preheated oven at 230°C/450°F/gas 8/fan oven 210°C for 30 minutes to brown and crisp. Remove from the oven and leave to stand for 10 minutes before carving.

6   Meanwhile, blend the flour with the water in a saucepan. Blend in the cooking juices from the stock pot, bring to the boil and cook, stirring, for 2 minutes. Season to taste, if necessary.

7   Carve the bird and serve with the gravy, stuffing and your usual accompaniments.

Serving tip
• Use any leftover meat chopped up and mixed with salad leaves for an easy lunch.

chicken in cider & cream

Chef's note

This is a glamorous dish even though it requires absolutely no effort. If you don't have any cider you can use apple juice instead or even a fruity white wine. Use any mixture of vegetables you like.

3 hrs HIGH or 6 hrs LOW

Rice

450 g/1 lb frozen steamable **mixed baby vegetables**, such as baby sweetcorn cobs, carrots, green beans

100 g/4 oz **fresh button** or **frozen sliced mushrooms**

450 g/1 lb diced **chicken meat**

45 ml/3 tbsp **cornflour** (cornstarch)

Salt and freshly ground black pepper

30 ml/2 tbsp **dried onion flakes**

150 ml/¼ pt/⅔ cup medium-dry **cider**

150 ml/¼ pint/⅔ cup boiling **chicken stock**

1 **bouquet garni sachet**

90 ml/6 tbsp **double (heavy) cream**

30 ml/2 tbsp chopped fresh or frozen **parsley**

1   Put all the ingredients except the cream and parsley in the crock pot and mix together thoroughly.

2   Cover and cook on High for 3 hours or Low for 6 hours.

3   Discard the bouquet garni and stir in the cream. Taste and re-season, if necessary.

4   Serve on a bed of rice, garnished with the chopped parsley.

Serving tip

• There are some delicious dry ciders on the market now, which would make a lovely drink to serve with this dish.

chicken in red wine

4

3 hrs HIGH or **6** hrs LOW

Creamed potatoes or rice and green beans

Chef's note

Based on the classic French dish coq au vin, this is just a doddle to make! You can make it with white wine instead of red, but make sure it's a fruity one that's not too dry.

A good handful of **frozen diced onion**, or 1 **fresh onion**, chopped

10 ml/2 tsp softened **butter**

100 g/4 oz smoked **lardons** (diced bacon)

4 skinless **chicken breasts**

100 g/4 oz baby **button mushrooms**, or 1 x 300 g/ 11 oz/medium can of **button mushrooms**, drained

300 ml/½ pt/1¼ cups **red wine**

15 ml/1 tbsp **tomato purée** (paste)

45 ml/3 tbsp **cornflour** (cornstarch)

30 ml/2 tbsp **brandy**

250 ml/8 fl oz/1 cup boiling **chicken stock**

5 ml/1 tsp **caster (superfine) sugar**

2.5 ml/½ tsp **dried mixed herbs**

Salt and freshly ground black pepper

A little chopped fresh **parsley** to garnish

1 Mix the onion with the butter in the crock pot. Sprinkle the lardons over, then add the chicken and mushrooms.

2 Blend the wine with the tomato purée and cornflour until smooth, then stir in the brandy, stock, sugar and herbs. Pour over the chicken and season with salt and pepper.

3 Cover and cook on High for 3 hours or Low for 6 hours until the sauce is rich and the chicken tender. Stir well. Taste and re-season, if necessary.

4 Garnish with a little chopped parsley.

5 Serve with creamed potatoes or rice and green beans.

Serving tip
• Try to choose local vegetables in season when you can. You'll be rewarded with much better flavours.

a taste of tandoori

Chef's note

Real tandoori chicken is baked in a tandoor – a clay oven that slightly chars the chicken. This is not intended to be anything like that. Here the chicken is cooked slowly and gently to tender succulence but with no charring. You can use whole chicken portions, but you'll need to pull off as much skin as possible before coating in the tandoori mixture.

4

3 hrs HIGH or **6** hrs LOW

Rice, mango chutney and a green salad

120 ml/4 fl oz/½ cup **Greek-style strained yoghurt**

45 ml/3 tbsp **tandoori paste** from a jar

5 ml/1 tsp chopped fresh or thawed frozen **coriander** (cilantro)

8 boned skinless **chicken thighs**

Wedges of **lime** to garnish (optional)

1   Mix together all the ingredients except the chicken and the wedges of lime for garnish in the crock pot.

2   Make several slashes in the chicken flesh by snipping with scissors or using a sharp knife. Place in the crock pot, open out and turn over so they are coated in the mixture. Rub it well into the slits, using your fingers, then reshape into thighs.

3   Cover and cook on High for 2–3 hours or Low for 4–6 hours until tender.

4   Lift the chicken out of the pot with tongs or a draining spoon. Transfer to plates, garnish with wedges of lime, if liked.

5   Serve with rice, mango chutney and a green salad.

Serving tip

- Another tasty accompaniment is a salad of chopped cucumber and onion, flavoured with mint.

thai green chicken curry

4

3 hrs HIGH
or **6** hrs LOW

Rice or egg noodles

A good handful of **frozen diced onion**, or 1 **fresh onion** or 4 **spring onions** (scallions), chopped

10 ml/2 tsp softened **butter**

450 g/1 lb diced **chicken**

200 g/7 oz **frozen green beans**, cut into short lengths

400 g/14 oz/1 large can of **coconut milk**

45 ml/3 tbsp **Thai green curry paste**

5 ml/1 tsp **lemon grass** from a jar

15 ml/1 tbsp **Thai fish sauce** (nam pla)

Salt and freshly ground black pepper

A few **dried chives** to garnish

1   Mix the onion with the butter in the crock pot. Add the chicken and beans and spread out.

2   Mix the coconut milk with the curry paste, lemon grass and fish sauce. Pour over the chicken and beans.

3   Cover and cook on High for 3 hours or Low for 6 hours until really tender.

4   Taste and re-season, if necessary.

5   Spoon over rice or egg noodles and serve sprinkled with a few dried chives.

Cook's tip

• If you like extra heat, add some chopped chillies from a jar, some crushed dried chillies or some slices of pickled jalapeño pepper to the coconut milk mixture.

chinese chicken curry

4

3 hrs HIGH
or **6** hrs LOW

Rice

Chef's note

This is so easy and quick to put together and is delicious just accompanied by rice. You can use a packet of ready-prepared fresh or frozen stir-fry vegetables for quickness or, of course, you could prepare your own from scratch.

A good handful of **frozen diced onion**, or 1 **fresh onion**, chopped

15 ml/1 tbsp **sunflower oil**

450 g/1 lb diced **chicken meat**

45 ml/3 tbsp **cornflour** (cornstarch)

A handful of **frozen sliced mixed (bell) peppers**, or 1 large fresh **pepper**, sliced

100 g/4 oz fresh or frozen baby **sweetcorn cobs** (8–10)

200 ml/7 fl oz/scant 1 cup boiling **chicken stock**

10 ml/2 tsp **chopped garlic** from a jar, or 2 **garlic cloves**, chopped

15 ml/1 tbsp **mild curry powder**

10 ml/2 tsp **light brown sugar**

30 ml/2 tbsp **soy sauce**

Salt

1   Mix the onion with the oil in the crock pot.

2   Toss the chicken in the cornflour and place in the crock pot with any remaining cornflour. Scatter the peppers and sweetcorn cobs over.

3   Blend the stock with all the remaining ingredients and pour over.

4   Cover and cook on High for 3 hours or Low for 6 hours until the chicken is really tender and the sauce is thick.

5   Stir gently, taste and re-season if necessary, remember soy sauce is salty.

6   Serve spooned over rice.

Serving tip

• I also like to serve this with stir-fried vegetables, flavoured with soy sauce and grated fresh root ginger.

barbecued chicken wings

4

3 hrs HIGH
or 6 hrs LOW

Jacket potatoes
and a green
salad

90 ml/6 tbsp **smoky barbecue table sauce**

30 ml/2 tbsp **clear honey**

60 ml/4 tbsp **tomato purée** (paste)

30 ml/2 tbsp **soy sauce**

16 **chicken wings**, about 1 kg/2¼ lb

Chef's note

Chicken wings cook really well in the slow cooker. I would normally cut off the wing tips at the first joint and discard them but you don't have to prepare them at all if you prefer not to. You can also pop them under the grill or on the barbecue to crisp and brown at the end, but they are delicious, moist and tender straight out of the pot.

1   Mix together all the ingredients except the chicken. Line the crock pot with foil, if liked (to help keep it clean).

2   Add the wings to the pot, spoon the sauce over and turn to coat them completely in the mixture. Spread them out evenly.

3   Cover and cook on High for 2–3 hours or Low for 4–6 hours until the wings are tender and coated in a rich sauce, turning and rearranging the chicken once for best results.

4   Serve with jacket potatoes and a green salad.

Serving tip

- Very messy – provide your diners with plenty of paper napkins and perhaps a finger bowl.

hot pepper pot with couscous

4

4 hrs HIGH or **8** hrs LOW

A green salad

Chef's note

This recipe has a fiery sweet flavour. If you prefer less heat, use less chilli. A simple green salad makes an ideal accompaniment, though you could equally well serve it with just plain potatoes, instead of couscous.

8 small or 4 large **skinless chicken thighs**

4 **belly pork slices**, halved

A good handful of **frozen diced onion**, or 1 **fresh onion**, chopped

2 large handfuls of **frozen sliced mixed (bell) peppers**, or 1 red and 1 green fresh **pepper**, sliced

2.5 ml/½ tsp **chopped chillies** from a jar or **dried crushed chillies**

15 ml/1 tbsp **light brown sugar**

2.5 ml/½ tsp **ground cinnamon**

A good pinch of **ground cloves**

2.5 ml/½ tsp **dried thyme**

10 ml/2 tsp **red wine vinegar**

300 ml/½ pt/1¼ cups boiling **chicken stock**

Salt and freshly ground black pepper

225 g/8 oz/1⅓ cups **couscous**

1   Put the chicken, pork, onion, peppers and chillies in the crock pot.

2   Blend together all the remaining ingredients except the couscous and pour over, seasoning with some salt and lots of pepper.

3   Cover and cook on High for 4 hours or Low for 8 hours until everything is tender.

4   Gently stir in the couscous, re-cover and leave on Low for 5 minutes while the couscous absorbs the stock.

5   Gently fluff up the couscous with a fork and serve in bowls.

6   Accompany with a green salad.

Serving tip

• You could also accompany this with rice with some diced avocado, tomato and cucumber stirred into it.

sherried chicken with peppers

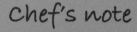

4

3 hrs HIGH
or **6** hrs LOW

Pasta and a
green salad

Chef's note

This has been a firm favourite in my family for many years. You can ring the changes by substituting the same quantity of cider, wine or vermouth if you don't usually keep sherry in the house – certainly don't go out and buy a bottle specially!

2 good handfuls of **frozen sliced mixed (bell) peppers**, or 1 red and 1 green fresh **pepper**, sliced

12 baby **button mushrooms**

30 ml/2 tbsp **dried onion flakes**

2.5 ml/½ tsp **chopped garlic** from a jar, or 1 small **garlic clove**, chopped

400 g/14 oz/large can of **chopped tomatoes**

45 ml/3 tbsp **dry sherry**

30 ml/2 tbsp **tomato purée** (paste)

2.5 ml/½ tsp **dried mixed herbs**

5 ml/1 tsp **caster (superfine) sugar**

4 skinless **chicken breasts**

Salt and freshly ground black pepper

1   Put the peppers, mushrooms, onion and garlic in the crock pot and pour the tomatoes over.

2   Blend the sherry with the tomato purée and add to the crock pot with the herbs and sugar. Stir well. Add the chicken breasts, pushing them well down in the sauce. Season with salt and pepper.

3   Cover and cook on High for 3 hours or Low for 6 hours until everything is tender and well flavoured.

4   Serve with pasta and a green salad

Serving tip

• This is equally delicious served with potatoes and broccoli or peas.

chicken, chorizo & barley paella

4

2 hrs HIGH
or **4** hrs LOW

Garlic bread and a crisp green salad

350 g/12 oz/ generous 1⅔ cups **pearl barley**

15 ml/1 tbsp **olive oil**

A handful of **frozen sliced mixed (bell) peppers**, or 1 red fresh **pepper**, sliced

12 baby **button mushrooms**

A handful of **frozen diced onion**, or 1 **fresh onion**, chopped

5 ml/1 tsp **chopped garlic** from a jar, or 1 **garlic clove**, chopped

100 g/4 oz ready-diced **chorizo**

8 small skinless **chicken thighs**

2.5 ml/½ tsp **pimentón** (smoked paprika)

2.5 ml/½ tsp **ground turmeric**

5 ml/1 tsp **dried oregano**

900 ml/1½ pts/3¾ cups boiling **chicken stock**

Salt and freshly ground black pepper

30 ml/2 tbsp chopped fresh **parsley**

Lemon wedges to garnish

1   Put the barley and oil in the crock pot and stir so it is well coated.

2   Add the peppers, mushrooms, onion, garlic and chorizo.

3   Tuck in the pieces of chicken.

4   Stir the spices and herbs into the stock and season with salt and pepper. Pour into the pot.

5   Cover and cook on High for 2 hours or Low for 4 hours until the barley has absorbed the liquid and the chicken is tender.

6   Stir well, taste and re–season, then spoon into bowls, sprinkle with parsley and garnish with lemon wedges.

7   Serve with garlic bread and a crisp green salad.

Cook's tips

- You can use chunks of chicken if you prefer.
- You can, of course, buy a piece of chorizo and chop it yourself.

creamy coconut chicken

Chef's note

In its homeland of Vietnam, this is quite a fiery dish. Mine is a milder and more subtle version, perfect to enjoy with a glass of cold lager. If you like your food spicier, try adding one or two seeded and chopped fresh green chillies to the sauce; the result will be fabulous.

4

3 hrs HIGH
or **6** hrs LOW

Rice

30 ml/2 tbsp **sunflower oil**

A handful of **frozen diced onion**, or 1 **fresh onion**, chopped

10 ml/2 tsp **chopped garlic** from a jar, or 2 **garlic cloves**, chopped

450 g/1 lb diced **chicken**

10 ml/2 tsp **ground turmeric**

5 ml/1 tsp **ground ginger**

5 ml/1 tsp **ground cumin**

5 ml/1 tsp **lemon grass** from a jar

100 g/4 oz **creamed coconut**

300 ml/½ pt/1¼ cups boiling **water**

Salt and freshly ground black pepper

45 ml/3 tbsp **single (light) cream**

50 g/2 oz/½ cup **roasted peanuts**, chopped

A handful of torn fresh **coriander** (cilantro) leaves

1   Mix the oil, onion and garlic in the crock pot and place the chicken on top.

2   Stir the spices and coconut into the boiling water, breaking up the coconut and mixing until most of the coconut has melted. Then pour over the ingredients in the pot. Season with salt and pepper.

3   Cover and cook on High for 2–3 hours or Low for 4–6 hours.

4   Stir in the cream, taste and re–season, if necessary.

5   Serve over rice, sprinkled with the chopped peanuts and torn coriander leaves.

Cook's tip
• For added elegance, you could sprinkle the dish with whole cashews instead of the chopped peanuts.

chicken tagine with prunes

4

3 hrs HIGH
or **6** hrs LOW

Crisp green salad

Chef's note

This popular casserole is good served with bulghar (cracked wheat) as a change from couscous. I like to cook the grains, then mix in a handful each of fresh chopped parsley, coriander and mint, some seasoning and a drizzle of olive oil. Serve with a crisp green salad to offset the richness.

15 ml/1 tbsp **olive oil**

2 large handfuls of **frozen diced onion**, or 2 **fresh onions**, chopped

A handful of **frozen sliced mixed (bell) pepper**s, or 1 red fresh **pepper**, sliced

8 ready-to-eat stoned (pitted) **prunes**, halved

4 **chicken portions**, skinned

1 small **lemon**, halved

5 ml/1 tsp **ground cinnamon**

2.5 ml/½ tsp **dried oregano**

30 ml/2 tbsp **thick honey**

30 ml/2 tbsp **tomato purée** (paste)

300 ml/½ pt /1¼ cups boiling **chicken stock**

Salt and freshly ground black pepper

50 g/2 oz/½ cup **blanched (slivered) almonds**

30 ml/2 tbsp **sesame seeds**, toasted

1   Put the oil, onions, peppers and prunes in the crock pot.

2   Trim off all excess fat from the chicken and rub all over with the lemon. Place in the pot.

3   Stir the cinnamon, oregano, honey and tomato purée into the hot stock, then pour into the crock pot and season with salt and pepper.

4   Cover and cook on High for 3 hours or Low for 6 hours until the meat is very tender.

5   Taste and re–season, if necessary, and sprinkle with the almonds and sesame seeds.

6   Serve with a green salad.

Cook's tip

• Don't be put off by the prunes if you are not usually a fan. They give this dish a lovely rich flavour.

caribbean chicken loaf

4

3 hrs HIGH
or **6** hrs LOW

Prawn crackers

Chef's note

This makes a great summer dish and is ridiculously simple to make. You can spice it up with a good pinch of chilli powder or change the flavour by adding a teaspoonful of root ginger from a jar or ground ginger instead of the five-spice powder.

For the loaf:

2 **pimientos** (sweet red peppers) from a can or jar, drained

350 g/12 oz/3 cups **minced (ground) chicken or turkey**

5 ml/1 tsp **chopped garlic** from a jar, or 1 **garlic clove**, chopped

440 g/15½ oz/large can of **crushed pineapple**

2 x 40 g/1½ oz packets of **bread sauce mix**

30 ml/2 tbsp **soy sauce**

5 ml/1 tsp **Chinese five-spice powder**

2 **eggs**, beaten

Salt and freshly ground black pepper

For the salad:

300 g/11 oz packet of ready-prepared **stir-fry vegetables**

15 ml/1 tbsp **sunflower oil**

30 ml/2 tbsp **soy sauce**

15 ml/1 tbsp **balsamic vinegar**

1   To make the loaf, put the pimientos in a large bowl and mash roughly with a fork. Add the all remaining loaf ingredients and mix together thoroughly.

2   Turn the mixture into a greased 450 g/1 lb loaf tin and cover with foil. Place in the crock pot and pour round enough boiling water to come half-way up the sides of the tin.

3   Cover and cook on High for 3 hours or Low for 6 hours until cooked through and firm to the touch.

4   Remove from the cooker and leave to cool.

5   To prepare the salad, put the vegetables in a bowl, sprinkle the oil, soy sauce and balsamic vinegar over and toss well.

6   Turn out the loaf on to a serving plate and slice.

7   Serve warm or cold with the salad and plenty of prawn crackers.

Serving tip

• This loaf is ideal for picnics, sliced and individually wrapped.

chicken & coconut curry

Chef's note

This is really easy and tastes very good. Apart from rice, I love to serve this curry with lots of popadoms, some minted yoghurt and a side salad.

4

3 hrs HIGH
or **6** hrs LOW

Rice

A good handful of **frozen diced onion**, or 1 **fresh onion**, chopped

550 g /1¼ lb diced **chicken**

45 ml/3 tbsp **raisins**

½ block of **creamed coconut**

300 ml/½ pt/1¼ cups boiling **chicken stock**

30 ml/2 tbsp mild **curry paste**

5 ml/1 tsp **ground turmeric**

5 ml/1 tsp **caster (superfine) sugar**

10 ml/2 tsp chopped **coriander** (cilantro), fresh, frozen or from a jar

Salt and freshly ground black pepper

1   Put the onion, chicken and raisins in the crock pot.

2   Add the creamed coconut to the boiling stock and break up and stir until partially melted (it doesn't matter if there are a few lumps). Stir in the curry paste, turmeric and sugar. Pour over the chicken.

3   Cover and cook on High for 3 hours or Low for 6 hours until the chicken is tender and the sauce is thick.

4   Stir in the coriander and season to taste.

5   Serve spooned on a bed of rice.

Cook's tip

• Cook popadoms in the microwave one at a time for about 45 seconds, turning once until puffed.

ginger soy duck with noodles

4

5-6 hrs
LOW

Prawn crackers

Chef's note

Packets of ready-prepared stir-fry vegetables vary enormously in size. However, I recommend that you use the biggest your family will eat as it's a great way to get some of their five a day into them! I like to use ones that include crunchy beansprouts, but the choice is yours.

60 ml/4 tbsp **soy sauce**, plus extra for sprinkling

30 ml/2 tbsp **boiling water**

30 ml/2 tbsp **light brown sugar**

10 ml/2 tsp **root ginger** from a jar, or use freshly grated

5 ml/1 tsp **chopped garlic** from a jar, or 1 **garlic clove**, chopped

A good pinch of **Chinese five-spice powder**

4 **duck portions**

4 slabs of dried **Chinese egg noodles**, or 300 g/11 oz fresh

400 g/14 oz packet of fresh or thawed frozen **stir-fry vegetables** with red (bell) peppers

1   Mix together the soy sauce, boiling water, sugar, ginger, garlic and five-spice powder in the crock pot. Add the duck and turn to coat completely in the marinade.

2   Cover and cook on Low for 5–6 hours until tender.

3   Just before the end of the cooking time, reconstitute the noodles, if using dried, according to the packet directions and drain.

4   When the duck is cooked, carefully lift the portions out of the pot. Spoon off all the excess fat and add the vegetables and noodles to the pot. Toss well.

5   Put the duck back on top, cover and leave for 10 more minutes.

6   Spoon into large bowls and serve with extra soy sauce sprinkled over and prawn crackers.

Serving tip
• Soy sauce can be quite salty, so taste when you sprinkle on the extra for serving.

oriental turkey wraps

Chef's note

This is a tasty alternative to roast Peking duck. The turkey is slow cooked in a soy marinade until meltingly tender and then served in flour tortillas, rather than the more usual thin Chinese pancakes. It's more filling for a complete meal and takes far less work.

4

3 hrs HIGH
or **6** hrs LOW

450 g/1 lb **turkey stir-fry pieces**

For the marinade:

30 ml/2 tbsp **soy sauce**

5 ml/1 tsp **root ginger** from a jar, or use freshly grated

5 ml/1 tsp **chopped garlic** from a jar, or 1 **garlic clove**, chopped

15 ml/1 tbsp **red wine vinegar**

10 ml/2 tsp **light or dark brown sugar**

To finish:

12 flour **tortillas**

1 jar of **hoisin sauce**

300 g/11 oz packet of ready-prepared fresh **stir-fry vegetables with beansprouts**

1   Put the turkey in the crock pot. Mix together the marinade ingredients and pour over the turkey. Stir well.

2   Cover and cook on High for 3 hours or Low for 6 hours.

3   When you are almost ready to serve up, warm the tortillas according to the packet directions. Put the hoisin sauce in one bowl and the stir-fry vegetables in another.

4   Tip the turkey mixture into a warm serving dish.

5   To serve, spread a little hoisin sauce on a tortilla, add some vegetables and top with some turkey. Roll up and enjoy.

Cook's tip

• This is good made with chicken instead of turkey.

game pie with port

4

4 hrs HIGH or **8** hrs LOW

Baby potatoes and broccoli

Chef's note

Frozen mixed diced game is now available in many good supermarkets, but you can also use diced beef or venison in this recipe. The meat is gently cooked with vegetables, herbs and spices, then topped with crisp puff pastry at the last minute.

340 g/13 oz packet of **frozen game casserole meat**, thawed

225 g/8 oz **frozen casserole vegetables**

100 g/4 z **whole baby button or frozen sliced mushrooms**

30 ml/2 tbsp **plain (all-purpose) flour**

5 ml/1 tsp **ground cinnamon**

A good pinch of **ground cloves**

5 ml/1 tsp **chopped garlic** from a jar, or 1 **garlic clove**, chopped

1 **bay leaf**

15 ml/1 tbsp **tomato purée (paste)**

150 ml/¼ pt/⅔ cup **port**

150 ml/¼ pt/⅔ cup **passata** (sieved tomatoes)

5 ml/1 tsp **caster (superfine) sugar**

15 ml/1 tbsp **brandy** (optional)

150 ml/¼ pt/⅔ cup **chicken or beef stock**

Salt and freshly ground black pepper

1 sheet of ready-rolled **puff pastry** (paste)

120 ml/4 fl oz/½ cup **single (light) cream**

1   Mix together everything except the pastry and cream in the crock pot, seasoning well.

2   Cover and cook on High for 3–4 hours or Low for 6–8 hours until really tender and richly flavoured.

3   When nearly ready to serve, preheat the oven to 220°C/425°F/gas 7/fan oven 200°C. Cut the sheet of pastry in quarters and transfer to a dampened baking (cookie) sheet.

4   Lightly score the pastry in a criss-cross pattern with the back of a knife, then brush with a little of the cream. Bake in the oven for about 8 minutes or until golden and crisp.

5   Gently stir the remaining cream into the casserole, taste and re-season if necessary.

6   Spoon on to plates, top each with a piece of pastry and serve with baby potatoes and broccoli.

Serving tip
• You can also serve this as a casserole without the pastry topping.

Cook's tip
• You can also make this with duck.

beef dishes

Like chicken with skin, beef is often browned before cooking to give it an appetising colour and a richer flavour. But here I've created some clever taste and colour combinations that mean you don't have to bother with all that frying first. The long, slow cooking helps impart more depth of flavour than conventional cooking and tenderises the meat beautifully, too – so it's a win-win situation! I would normally buy a piece of well-hung stewing steak and prepare it myself but, in the spirit of the book, I've tested these with ready-prepared meat. I recommend you choose carefully. Make sure what you buy is lean, cut into even sized pieces and does not have great chunks of gristle. It's worth buying the best quality you can afford, ideally from British cattle.

Tips for great slow-cooked beef

- Cheaper cuts of beef are ideal for slow cooking as they tenderise beautifully.

- Always defrost frozen meat thoroughly before cooking (except free-flow mince, which can be cooked from frozen).

- Trim any excess fat from beef before slow cooking.

- Use a good-quality free-flow mince for best results.

- Meat should always go on top of the vegetables when cooking meat and root vegetables together, as they will take longer to cook than the meat.

- Beef cooks well in beer or red wine. Substitute it for half the liquid in a recipe.

- You can always add a little extra liquid at the end of cooking if the sauce is too thick.

- You can adapt your usual casserole recipes by cutting down the liquid content by 30–50 per cent or by increasing the flour or cornflour (cornstarch) thickener by a third.

chunky chilli con carne

4

5-6 hrs

HIGH

Shredded lettuce and flour tortillas

Chef's note

Instead of the usual frying off then simmering on top of the stove, here you can just throw it all in and leave it. It's so good to think all day about coming home to a bowl of chilli, only needing to be topped with grated cheese before eating with shredded lettuce and lots of flour tortillas, rolled up to use instead of ordinary bread to help shovel it on to your fork.

A good handful of **frozen diced onion**, or 1 **fresh onion**, chopped

15 ml/1 tbsp **olive oil**

450 g/1 lb lean diced **stewing steak**

2 x 400 g/14 oz/large cans of **red kidney beans**, drained

200 ml/7 fl oz/scant 1 cup **passata** (sieved tomatoes)

¼ x 200 g/7 oz jar of **pickled sliced jalapeño peppers**, drained

2.5 ml/½ tsp hot **chilli powder** (or to taste)

5 ml/1 tsp **ground cumin**

5 ml/1 tsp **dried oregano**

5 ml/1 tsp **caster (superfine) sugar**

Salt and freshly ground black pepper

Grated cheese and a little **soured (dairy sour) cream** to garnish

1   Mix together the onion and oil in the crock pot. Add all the remaining ingredients except the grated cheese and soured cream garnish and stir well.

2   Cover and cook on High for 5–6 hours until meltingly tender.

3   Taste and re-season, if necessary. Top with grated cheese and a spoonful of soured cream.

4   Serve with shredded lettuce and lots of flour tortillas.

Cook's tip

• Adjust the chilli seasoning to suit your taste.

beef stew with tomatoes

5 hrs HIGH or
10 hrs LOW

Rice and a green salad

This recipe is based on a classic French dish I have done in the slow cooker before but this version doesn't have any frying or grating. I recommend you keep a tube of anchovy paste in the fridge. It adds a fabulous depth of flavour to numerous savoury dishes.

A good handful of **frozen diced onion**, or 1 **large onion**, chopped

15 ml/1 tbsp **olive oil**

100 g/4 oz **unsmoked lardons** (diced bacon)

1 kg/2¼ lb diced **braising steak**

10 ml/2 tsp **chopped garlic** from a jar, or 1 large **garlic clove**, chopped

225 g/8 oz fresh or frozen **baby carrots**

225 g/8 oz fresh or frozen diced **butternut squash**

400 g/14 oz/1 large can of **chopped tomatoes**

10 ml/2 tsp **anchovy paste** (optional)

300 ml/½ pint/1¼ cups **red wine**

60 ml/4 tbsp pure **orange juice**

15 ml/1 tbsp **tomato purée** (paste)

5 ml/1 tsp **dried rosemary**

Salt and freshly ground black pepper

16 **black olives in oil**, drained

1   Mix together the onion and oil in the crock pot. Add all the
    remaining ingredients and stir well.

2   Cover and cook on High for 4–5 hours or Low for 8–10 hours
    until the meat is meltingly tender and bathed in a rich sauce.
    Taste and re-season, if necessary.

3   Serve with rice and a green salad.

Cook's tip

• Anchovy paste has a strong flavour, so err on the side of caution if
you haven't used it before.

thai red beef curry & cashews

4

5 hrs HIGH or
10 hrs LOW

Jasmine rice

A good handful of **frozen diced onion**, or 1 **fresh onion**, chopped

5 ml/1 tsp **chopped garlic** from a jar, or 1 **garlic clove**, chopped

700 g/1½ lb lean diced **stewing steak**

12 washed **small potatoes**

45 ml/3 tbsp **Thai red curry paste**

5 ml/1 tsp **caster (superfine) sugar**

400 g/14 oz/1 large can of **coconut milk**

Salt and freshly ground black pepper

8 slices of **pickled red or green chilli**, drained

50 g/2 oz/½ cup raw **cashew nuts**

4 **tomatoes**, quartered

A few torn **coriander (cilantro) leaves** and wedges of **lemon** to garnish

1   Put all the ingredients except the cashew nuts, tomatoes and coriander and lemon garnish in the crock pot and stir well.

2   Cover and cook on High for 5 hours or Low for 10 hours until everything is meltingly tender.

3   Add the cashew nuts and tomatoes and leave for 5 minutes.

4   Serve spooned over jasmine rice in bowls, each serving garnished with a few coriander leaves and a wedge of lemon.

Cook's tip

- You can omit the cashew nuts, if you prefer, but they do add great flavour and texture to the dish.

hot & sweet beef with beans

4

5 hrs HIGH or **10** hrs LOW

Crusty bread

Chef's note

In Asia they use daikon in this type of dish, which is also known as winter radish. You can buy it in the UK but it needs preparing for use, so here I've used the round pink radishes, which impart a very similar flavour, look really attractive and mean no work.

A good handful of **frozen diced onion**, or 1 **fresh onion**, chopped

½ packet of pink round **radishes** (no need to trim)

2 handfuls (about 16) of fresh or frozen **baby carrots**

12 small **new potatoes**, scrubbed

2 handfuls (about 100 g/4 oz) of frozen **soya beans**

550 g/1¼ lb lean diced **stewing steak**

10 ml/2 tsp **chopped garlic** from a jar, or 2 **garlic cloves**, chopped

5 ml/1 tsp mild **curry powder or paste**

10 ml/2 tsp **root ginger** from a jar, or use freshly grated

A 5 cm/2 in piece of **cinnamon stick**

1 **star anise**

2.5 ml/½ tsp crushed **dried chillies**

1 **bay leaf**

30 ml/2 tbsp **tomato purée** (paste)

5 ml/1 tsp **light brown sugar**

200 ml/7 fl oz/scant 1 cup boiling **beef stock**

Salt and freshly ground black pepper

A few **dried chives** to garnish

1   Put the vegetables, beans and beef in the crock pot. Add all the remaining ingredients except the chive garnish, adding a little salt and a good grinding of pepper.

2   Cover and cook on High for 4–5 hours or Low for 8–10 hours until the beef is meltingly tender.

3   Discard the cinnamon stick and star anise, taste and re-season if necessary.

4   Serve in large open soup bowls, garnished with the chives, with crusty bread to accompany.

Cook's tip

• Use canned or frozen baby broad (fava) beans instead of frozen soya beans, if you prefer.

minced beef curry

4

3 hrs HIGH
or **6** hrs LOW

Rice and mango chutney

Chef's note

This is a mild curry based on keema curry, which is enjoyed all over India. I added the cream at the end to make it richer, but you don't have to include it.

450 g/1 lb freeflow frozen **minced (ground) beef**

30 ml/2 tbsp **sunflower oil**

2 large handfuls of **frozen diced onion**, or 2 **fresh onions**, chopped

10 ml/2 tsp **chopped garlic** from a jar, or 2 **garlic cloves**, chopped

10 ml/2 tsp **root ginger** from a jar, or use freshly grated

30 ml/2 tbsp **curry powder**

30 ml/2 tbsp **tomato purée** (paste)

200 ml/7 fl oz/scant 1 cup **boiling water**

Salt

60 ml/4 tbsp **double (heavy) cream** (optional)

1   Put the beef, oil, onions, garlic and ginger into the crock pot
    and stir well.

2   Stir the curry powder and tomato purée into the hot water,
    then pour into the pot and season with salt.

3   Cover and cook on High for 2–3 hours or LOW for 4–6 hours
    until tender with a thick sauce.

4   Taste and re–season, if necessary, and stir in the cream,
    if using.

5   Serve with plain rice and mango chutney.

Serving tip

• If you don't want to add the cream, serve with a dollop of plain yoghurt.

kofta beefballs with mango

2 hrs HIGH
or **4** hrs LOW

Rice and a
tomato salad

Chef's note

Koftas are often made with minced lamb, which you can use instead if you prefer. Instead of grilling them, I've gently poached them in yoghurt stock, which keeps them really moist and succulent. Use strained Greek-style yoghurt, not a set one, or you'll have curds remaining when the dish is cooked.

700 g/1½ lb lean **minced (ground) beef**

5 ml/1 tsp **chopped garlic** from a jar, or 1 **garlic clove**, chopped

15 ml/1 tbsp **garam masala**

Salt and freshly ground black pepper

1 **egg**, beaten

2 **bay leaves**

1 piece of **cinnamon stick**

2 **whole cloves**

90 ml/6 tbsp **boiling water**

90 ml/6 tbsp **Greek-style strained yoghurt**

For the sauce:

15 ml/1 tbsp **mango chutney**

150 ml/¼ pt/⅔ cup **Greek-style strained yoghurt**

10 ml/2 tsp **mint sauce** from a jar

A good pinch of **chilli powder** or **crushed dried chillies**

Opposite: Beef in Beer with Parsnips (see pages 108–9)

1   Mix the beef with the garlic, garam masala and a little salt and pepper. Work in the beaten egg to bind. With wet hands, shape the mixture into sausage shapes about 7.5 cm/3 in long. Place in the crock pot and tuck the bay leaves, cinnamon stick and cloves around.

2   Mix together the water and yoghurt until smooth, then spoon over the meat.

3   Cover and cook on High for 2 hours or Low for 4 hours until the meatballs are cooked through. (The liquid will look slightly unappetising but don't worry – you don't eat it!)

4   Meanwhile, to make the sauce, chop up any large pieces in the mango chutney, if necessary, and place in a bowl. Mix in the remaining ingredients. Chill until ready to serve.

5   When the koftas are cooked, gently lift them out of the liquid with a draining spoon and transfer to warm plates.

6   Serve with rice, the sauce and a tomato salad.

Serving tip

• To make this even more filling, serve with pitta bread.

beef & vegetable loaf

6

3 hrs HIGH
or 6 hrs LOW

Chinese egg noodles

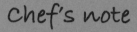

Chef's note

This is a fusion of basic American fare and Asian cuisine. It is simplicity itself to put together and makes a delicious meal served warm with some Chinese egg noodles, tossed in soy sauce and sesame seeds, or cold with a salad.

400 g/14 oz packet of fresh **stir-fry vegetables**

A pinch of **ground cinnamon**

450 g/1 lb lean **minced (ground) beef**

40 g/1½ packet of **bread sauce mix**

1 **egg**, beaten

120 ml/4 fl oz/½ cup **tomato or vegetable juice**

30 ml/2 tbsp **soy sauce**

To serve:

Sweet chilli dipping sauce from a bottle

1   Mix together all the ingredients and pack into a lightly greased 900 g/2 lb loaf tin. Cover with foil, twisting and folding under the rim to secure.

2   Place in the crock pot and pour round enough boiling water to come half-way up the sides of the tin.

3   Cover and cook on High for 3 hours or Low for 6 hours until cooked through and firm. Pour off the excess liquid and reserve.

4   Either leave to cool slightly then turn out and serve sliced with the juices spooned over and sweet chilli dipping sauce on the side, or leave to cool completely then weigh down with tins of food or weights and chill before serving (in which case, you could use the reserved juices to flavour a soup or sauce).

5   Serve with Chinese egg noodles as an accompaniment.

Cook's tip

• I find packets of shredded stir-fry vegetables are perfect for this and I also look out for ones that have been reduced for quick sale!

american-style meatloaf

4

4 hrs HIGH or **8** hrs LOW

Crusty bread and pickles

Any leftover loaf is delicious in sandwiches – or better still in chunks of crusty French bread with lots of salad and some mayonnaise, flavoured with tomato ketchup and Worcestershire sauce.

350 g/12 oz **lean minced (ground) beef**

½ x 85 g/3½ oz packet of **sage and onion stuffing mix**

175 ml/6 fl oz/¾ cup **passata** (sieved tomatoes) with onion

30 ml/2 tbsp **tomato ketchup** (catsup)

Salt and freshly ground black pepper

1 small **egg**, beaten

A little **oil** or **butter** for greasing

1   Mix the beef with the stuffing mix, 60 ml/4 tbsp of the passata, 15 ml/1 tbsp of the ketchup and some salt and pepper. Add the beaten egg and mix well to bind.

2   Turn the mixture into a greased 450 g/1 lb loaf tin and cover with foil, twisting and folding under the rim to secure. Place in the crock pot and pour round enough boiling water to come half-way up the sides of the tin.

3   Cook on High for 4 hours or Low for 8 hours.

4   Remove the tin from the crock pot, leave to cool slightly, then turn out on to a flameproof dish.

5   Meanwhile, heat the remaining passata with the remaining ketchup and a little salt and pepper.

6   Serve the loaf sliced with the tomato sauce spooned over, with crusty bread and pickles.

Cook's tip

• You could serve this with some bought barbecue sauce instead of the passata, if you prefer, or with potatoes and seasonal vegetables.

braised sweet-spiced beef

4

6 hrs HIGH or 12 hrs LOW

Rice

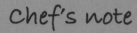

Chef's note

This is based on an Ethiopian dish called zigni. Even though it is simplicity itself to prepare, the finished dish is full of wonderful flavours.

15 ml/1 tbsp **olive oil**

2 large handfuls of **frozen diced onion**, or 2 **fresh onions**, chopped

10 ml/2 tsp **chopped garlic** from a jar, or 1 **large garlic clove**, chopped

400 g/14 oz/1 large can of **chopped tomatoes**

2 large handfuls of **frozen grilled (broiled) (bell) peppers**

450 g/1 lb thin–cut **beef frying steak**

15 ml/1 tbsp **tomato purée** (paste)

1.5 ml/¼ tsp **ground cloves**

2.5 ml/½ tsp **ground cumin**

2.5 ml/½ tsp **dried oregano**

150 ml/¼ pt/⅔ cup **boiling water**

Salt and freshly ground black pepper

30 ml/2 tbsp **chopped fresh parsley**

1   Mix the oil, onion, garlic, tomatoes and peppers in the crock pot. Add the meat.

2   Stir the tomato purée, spices and oregano into the boiling water and pour over these ingredients. Season with salt and pepper.

3   Cover and cook on High for 4–6 hours or LOW for 8–12 hours until the beef is really tender.

4   Taste and re–season, if necessary, and sprinkle with the parsley.

5   Serve with boiled rice.

Cook's tip

- In Ethiopia, they use different meats in this dish, so you can ring the changes with pork steaks or lamb chops.

chilli beef & tomato rice

4

2-3 hrs

LOW

Garden peas

Chef's note

This is a colourful all-in-one mince and rice supper dish, simmered in a rich tomato sauce spiced with chilli – delicious and almost unbelievably easy to put together.

225 g/8 oz freeflow frozen **minced (ground) beef**

A handful of **frozen diced onion**, or 1 **fresh onion**, chopped

250 ml/8 fl oz/1 cup **passata** (sieved tomatoes)

5 ml/1 tsp **chilli powder**

2.5 ml/½ tsp **dried mixed herbs**

Salt and freshly ground black pepper

120 ml/4 fl oz/½ cup **boiling beef stock**

175 g/6 oz/¾ cup **easy–cook (converted) rice**

200 g/7 oz/1 small can **sweetcorn**, drained

A handful of **frozen sliced mixed (bell) peppers**, or 1 red fresh **pepper**, sliced

1   Scatter about half of the minced beef evenly over the bottom of the crock pot. Top with about half of the onion, then sprinkle over the remaining beef, followed by the rest of the onion.

2   Stir the passata, stock, chilli powder, mixed herbs and some salt and pepper into the hot stock, then pour half over the beef and onion.

3   Sprinkle the rice evenly over the top, followed by the sweetcorn and pepper.

4   Pour over the remaining tomato sauce mixture.

5   Cover and cook on Low for 2–3 hours until the rice and beef are tender and most of the juices have been absorbed.

6   Serve straight away with garden peas.

Cook's tip

- It's important to use freeflow mince so it doesn't clump together in the pot. Minced pork or turkey could also be used in this dish.

beef with water chestnuts

4

5 hrs HIGH or
10 hrs LOW

Complete meal
in itself

Chef's note

I have done many versions of this dish in my time – it was introduced to me from South Africa by my mother-in-law many years ago. This one I have adapted for slow cooking convenience and the result is just great and doesn't need an accompaniment, though you could serve it with a green vegetable, if you like.

A good handful of **frozen diced onion**, or 1 **fresh onion**, chopped

16–24 washed **baby potatoes**

225 g/8 oz fresh or frozen **baby carrots**

1 x 225 g/8 oz/small can of **water chestnuts**, drained

100 g/4 oz fresh **baby button** or **frozen sliced mushrooms**

700 g/1½ lb lean diced **stewing steak**

60 ml/4 tbsp **plain (all-purpose) flour**

300 ml/½ pt/1¼ cups boiling **beef stock**

30 ml/2 tbsp **soy sauce**

Salt and freshly ground black pepper

295 g/10½ oz/medium can of **condensed cream of mushroom soup**

1   Mix together all the ingredients except the stock, soy sauce, seasoning and soup in the crock pot. Add the stock, soy sauce and seasoning and stir well. Spoon the soup over and spread it out.

2   Cover and cook on High for 5 hours or Low for 10 hours until the beef is meltingly tender and the soup has melted into the casserole.

3   Serve straight from the pot.

Cook's tip

• If you do serve with green vegetables, you'll get the best flavour if you choose vegetables in season. Why not try your local farmers' market?

beef in beer with parsnips

4

4 hrs HIGH
or **8** hrs LOW

Potatoes and
leafy greens

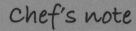

Chef's note

This is a lovely combination of flavours. The beer adds richness to the gravy and the prunes and parsnips impart a sweet, earthy depth. If you ever buy venison or rabbit, try cooking them in this way, too.

60 ml/4 tbsp **plain (all-purpose) flour**

Salt and freshly ground black pepper

1.5 ml/¼ tsp **mustard powder**

550 g/1¼ lb lean diced **stewing steak**

A good handful of **frozen diced onion**, or 1 **fresh onion**, chopped

225 g/8 oz (about 24 pieces) **frozen roasting parsnips**, or 1 large **parsnip**, cut into pieces

12 ready-to-eat **stoned (pitted) prunes**, halved

330 ml/½ pt/1¼ cup **brown beer**

150 ml/¼ pt/⅔ cup boiling **beef stock**

1 **bay leaf**

1   Mix the flour with some salt and pepper and the mustard powder in the crock pot. Add the meat and toss well to coat completely.

2   Add the onion, parsnips and prunes, then pour over the beer and stock. Stir well. Tuck in the bay leaf.

3   Cover and cook on High for 4 hours or Low for 8 hours until the beef is meltingly tender.

4   Stir gently, discard the bay leaf, taste and re-season, if necessary. Serve with potatoes and leafy greens.

Cook's tip

• If you aren't a prune lover, substitute raisins or leave them out altogether. The dish will be different but still tasty.

slow-roast silverside

4

5 hrs HIGH or
10 hrs LOW

Peas and horseradish
sauce and/or English
mustard

A good handful of **frozen diced onion**, or 1 **fresh onion**, chopped

200 g/7 oz fresh or frozen **baby carrots**

16–24 washed small **new potatoes**

1 **bay leaf**

1 kg/2¼ lb piece of **beef silverside**

Salt and freshly ground black pepper

2.5 ml/½ tsp **dried oregano**

450 ml/¾ pt/2 cups boiling **beef stock**

45 ml/3 tbsp **cornflour** (cornstarch)

45 ml/3 tbsp **water**

1   Put the onion, carrots and potatoes in the crock pot and spread out evenly. Add the bay leaf.

2   Put the beef on top of the vegetables and sprinkle with a little salt and pepper and the oregano. Pour the boiling stock around.

3   Cover and cook on High for 4–5 hours or Low for 8–10 hours. The meat should be very tender but still sliceable.

4   Transfer the meat to a carving dish and remove the vegetables with a draining spoon. Keep warm.

5   Turn the crock pot to High, if on Low. Blend together the cornflour and water and stir into the crock pot. Season to taste. Cover and leave to cook while you carve the meat.

6   Serve with the carrots and potatoes, some peas and the gravy spooned over. Offer horseradish sauce and/or mustard, as well.

Cook's tip
• You can serve with a leafy green vegetable, too, if you like.

lamb dishes

Lamb is a wonderful meat to slow cook because it can take on so many different flavourings and always remains tender and succulent. Some joints, particularly shoulder, can be a bit fatty, so choose carefully when you shop. Check before you put it in the pot, too, and, if you see large lumps of white fat, cut them off before you cook it. But, if you haven't time (and that's what this book is all about), you can spoon off the fat that will float to the surface before you serve the meal.

If any of you want to experiment, try using goat instead of lamb; it's lower in fat than any other meat and cooks beautifully in the slow cooker. It's not yet readily available in supermarkets, but can be found in some butchers and at farmers' markets and can also be bought online.

Opposite: French-style Lamb (see pages 124–5)

Tips for great slow-cooked lamb

- Always defrost frozen meat thoroughly before slow cooking.

- Trim off any fat from lamb before slow cooking.

- For best results, try to fill your crock pot reasonably full but not overfull. One chop in the pot, for example, will overcook unless the pot is filled up to at least a third with liquid.

- Meat should always go on top of the vegetables when cooking meat and root vegetables together, as they will take longer to cook than the meat.

- If you lift the lid often during cooking, you'll lose heat and may need to extend the cooking time. To check progress without lifting the lid, spin the lid until the condensation falls off, then it's easy to see inside.

braised lamb in garlic & tomato

4

4 hrs HIGH
or **8** hrs LOW

A green salad

Chef's note

Most cheat soup sauces are made with condensed varieties. Here I just use ordinary creamed soup. Once it's been simmering away with the lamb and little basil, the flavour is really rich.

4 lean **lamb shoulder steaks**

Salt and freshly ground black pepper

30 ml/2 tbsp **dried onion flakes**

2.5 ml/½ tsp **chopped garlic** from a jar, or 1 small **garlic clove**, chopped (optional)

400 g/14 oz/large can of **cream of tomato soup**

5 ml/1 tsp **dried basil**

350 g/12 oz **tagliatelle**

A few torn fresh **basil** or **parsley** leaves, to garnish (optional)

1   Season the steaks with a little salt and pepper, then arrange
    in the crock pot. Add the onion flakes and garlic, if using.
    Spoon the soup over and sprinkle with the dried basil.

2   Cover and cook on High for 3–4 hours or Low for 6–8 hours
    until the meat is really tender and bathed in sauce.

3   When nearly ready to serve, cook the tagliatelle according
    to the packet directions. Drain thoroughly.

4   Lift the lamb out of the crock pot. Add the tagliatelle to the
    sauce and toss well. Pile on to plates and top with the lamb.

5   Scatter the basil or parsley over, if using.

6   Serve with a large green salad.

Cook's tip
• You can use any kind of pasta as an accompaniment, or mashed
  potato is good, too.

italian-style slow-roast lamb

6

5 hrs HIGH or
10 hrs LOW

Ciabatta and a
green salad

Chef's note

Use the sort of Bolognese sauce usually added to minced (ground) beef for the popular spaghetti dish, but instead pour it over lamb for a glorious, rich, tomato-based sauce. This dish needs only lovely Italian bread and a fresh salad to round it off perfectly.

1 fresh or thawed frozen **boned and rolled shoulder of lamb**

500 ml/17 fl oz jar of **pasta sauce for Bolognese**

30 ml/2 tbsp sliced **black olives**

Salt and freshly ground black pepper

5 ml/1 tsp **chopped garlic** from a jar, or 1 **garlic clove**, chopped

2 x 350 g/12 oz/medium cans of **flageolet beans**, drained

15 ml/1 tbsp chopped fresh or frozen **parsley**

1   Put the lamb in the crock pot. Pour the sauce over and add the olives and garlic. Season with salt and pepper.

2   Cover and cook on High for 5 hours or Low for 10 hours until really tender.

3   Lift the lamb out of the sauce and put on a carving dish. Turn the cooker up to High, if on Low. Spoon any excess fat off the sauce and stir in the flageolet beans and parsley. Cover and leave to heat through while you carve the lamb into thick, chunky pieces.

4   Put the lamb in warm, shallow bowls and spoon the sauce over. Sprinkle each serving with the parsley and serve with ciabatta and a green salad.

Cook's tips
- Of course, the same sauce is ideal with other cuts of meat.
- Try using cannellini beans or chick peas (garbanzos) instead of flageolets.

creamy lamb & almond curry

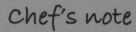

Chef's note

This tasty but mild korma curry is also lovely when made with chicken. Stirring in the garam masala at the end really lifts the whole thing and the coriander adds a lovely fragrance.

4

3 hrs HIGH
or **6** hrs LOW

Pilau rice and a green salad

700 g/1½ lb lean **diced lamb**

A handful of **frozen diced onion**, or 1 **fresh onion**, chopped

10 ml/2 tsp **chopped garlic** from a jar, or 2 **garlic cloves**, chopped

10 ml/2 tsp **root ginger** from a jar, or use freshly grated

50 g/2 oz/½ cup **ground almonds**

15 ml/1 tbsp **groundnut (peanut) oil**

4 **cardamom pods**, split

5 ml/1 tsp **ground cumin**

5 ml/1 tsp **ground coriander**

2.5 ml/½ tsp **ground cinnamon**

1.5 ml/¼ tsp hot **chilli powder**

A good pinch of **ground cloves**

10 ml/2 tsp **caster (superfine) sugar**

200 ml/7 fl oz/scant 1 cup boiling **water**

Salt and freshly ground black pepper

60 ml/4 tbsp **crème fraîche** or **single (light) cream**

2.5 ml/½ tsp **garam masala**

Wedges of **lemon** and torn **coriander (cilantro) leaves** to garnish

1   Mix the lamb onion, garlic, ginger, almonds and oil in the crock pot.

2   Stir the spices and sugar into the boiling water, pour over the ingredients and season with salt and pepper. Stir well.

3   Cover and cook on High for 3 hours or Low for 6 hours until the lamb is really tender.

4   Stir in the crème fraîche or cream and garam masala, taste and re–season, if necessary. Garnish with wedges of lemon and torn coriander leaves.

5   Serve with pilau rice and a green salad.

Serving tip

- You might also like to serve it with naan bread and a salad of chopped onion and cucumber, flavoured with mint.

lamb shanks & redcurrants

Chef's note

The fresh redcurrants in this recipe add a touch of tartness that offsets the richness of the meat. You'll need a large crock pot to accommodate the lamb.

4

8 hrs LOW

New potatoes and mangetout (snow peas)

Salt and freshly ground black pepper

4 **lamb shanks**

15 ml/1 tbsp chopped fresh **rosemary**

A good handful of **frozen diced onion**, or 1 **fresh onion**, chopped

45 ml/3 tbsp **port**

30 ml/2 tbsp **redcurrant jelly** (clear conserve)

200 ml/7 fl oz/scant 1 cup boiling **beef** or **chicken stock**

175 g/6 oz fresh **redcurrants**, plus a few extra sprigs to garnish

4 small sprigs of fresh **rosemary** to garnish

1   Season the lamb shanks, place in the crock pot and sprinkle with the rosemary. Add the onion.

2   Stir the port and redcurrant jelly into the hot stock, then pour over the meat.

3   Cover and cook on Low for 8 hours until meltingly tender.

4   Transfer the meat to a warm carving dish and keep warm. Reserve 4 small sprigs of redcurrants for garnish and remove the rest from their stalks with the prongs of a fork.

5   Spoon off any excess fat from the crock pot, turn it to High, then add the redcurrants and cook without a lid for about 5 minutes until the sauce is slightly reduced. Taste and re-season, if necessary.

6   Transfer the shanks to warm serving plates and spoon the redcurrant juices over. Garnish each chop with a small sprig of redcurrants and a sprig of rosemary.

7   Serve hot with new potatoes and mangetout.

Cook's tip
• You can use sweet sherry or Madeira if you prefer instead of port, which would add a richer flavour.

lamb tagine with apricots

4

4 hrs HIGH
or 8 hrs LOW

Couscous and a mixed salad

Chef's note

Using a can of apricots means you get extra lovely juice to flavour the sauce. But you can use ready-to-eat dried apricots instead and increase the stock by 150 ml/¼ pt/⅔ cup.

A good handful of **frozen diced onion**, or 1 **fresh onion**, chopped

700 g/1½ lb diced **stewing lamb**

5 ml/1 tsp **ground cinnamon**

5 ml/1 tsp **ground ginger**

5 ml/1 tsp **ground cumin**

2.5 ml/½ tsp **salt**

5 ml/1 tsp **chopped garlic** from a jar, or 1 **garlic clove**, chopped

Freshly ground black pepper

410 g/14 oz/large can of **apricot halves in natural juice**

30 ml/2 tbsp toasted **pine nuts**

30 ml/2 tbsp **tomato purée** (paste)

300 ml/½ pt/1¼ cups boiling **lamb** or **vegetable stock**

10 ml/2 tsp chopped fresh or frozen **coriander** (cilantro)

1 Put the onion in the crock pot and add the meat with all the spices, the salt, garlic and a good grinding of pepper. Stir well.

2 Add the apricots and their juice and the pine nuts. Blend the tomato purée into the stock and pour over. Stir, again very gently.

3 Cover and cook on High for 3–4 hours or Low for 6–8 hours until the lamb is really tender.

4 Stir in the coriander, taste and re-season, if necessary.

5 Serve with couscous and a mixed salad.

Cook's tips
- Make sure you use apricots in natural juice, not syrup.
- If you aren't a lover of apricots, add a large handful of raisins and increase the liquid by 150 ml/¼ pt/⅔ cup.

french-style lamb

4-5

5 hrs HIGH or
10 hrs LOW

Warm French bread

Chef's note

Lamb on the bone lends itself to slow cooking. This version has garlic, herbes de Provence and casserole vegetables all gently cooked in just a dash of red wine. It is simplicity itself, but the flavour is excellent.

450 g/1 lb **frozen casserole vegetables**, including celery and onion

½ small **leg of lamb**, about 700 g/ 1½ lb

450 g/1 lb washed **baby potatoes**

10 ml/2 tsp **chopped garlic** from a jar, or 1 large **garlic clove**, chopped

5 ml/1 tsp **dried herbes de Provence**

Salt and freshly ground black pepper

150 ml/¼ pt/⅔ cup boiling **lamb** or **chicken stock**

75 ml/5 tbsp **red wine**

A good pinch of **caster sugar**

1   Spread out the casserole vegetables in the crock pot. Put the lamb on top and surround with the potatoes.

2   Sprinkle the garlic and herbs over the lamb and season everything with a little salt and pepper.

3   Mix together the stock, wine and sugar and pour over the vegetables.

4   Cover and cook on High for 5 hours or Low for 10 hours or until everything is meltingly tender.

5   Cut the meat into chunks.

6   Serve in bowls with the vegetables and cooking juices and lots of warm French bread.

Cook's tip

• Herbes de provence is made from marjoram, thyme, savory, basil, rosemary, sage and fennel, so if you don't have any you could devise your own variation from whatever herbs you have to hand.

lamb in barbecue sauce

4-5

4 hrs HIGH or 8 hrs LOW

Rice and salad

Chef's note

This is a Greek–American dish – a delicious joint bathed in a dark, sticky barbecue sauce. It does have a little preparation, but it doesn't take long and I hope you will agree it is worth it.

½ **leg** or **shoulder of lamb**, about 1 kg/2¼ lb

30 ml/2 tbsp **lemon juice**

10 ml/2 tsp **chopped garlic** from a jar or 2 **garlic cloves**, cut in slivers

Salt and freshly ground black pepper

75 ml/5 tbsp **cider vinegar**

75 ml/5 tbsp **water**

45 ml/3 tbsp **golden (light corn) syrup**

30 ml/2 tbsp **tomato purée** (paste)

60 ml/4 tbsp **tomato ketchup** (catsup)

30 ml/2 tbsp **Worcestershire sauce**

1.5 ml/¼ tsp **chilli powder**

5 ml/1 tsp **onion granules**

15 ml/1 tbsp **cornflour** (cornstarch)

30 ml/2 tbsp chopped fresh **parsley** to garnish

1   Rub the lamb all over with lemon juice. Make small slits in the flesh and push in the chopped garlic or fresh slivers. Place in the crock pot.

2   Whisk all the remaining ingredients except the parsley garnish in a saucepan and bring to the boil, whisking, then spoon over the lamb.

3   Cover and cook on High for 3–4 hours or Low for 6–8 hours until the meat is meltingly tender.

4   Cut the meat into neat pieces, transfer to warm plates and spoon the juices over. Garnish with parsley.

5   Serve with rice and a large green salad.

Serving tip

• Try it, too, packed into warm pitta bread pockets with some shredded lettuce and cucumber, and minted yoghurt.

three-meat casserole

4

5 hrs HIGH or
10 hrs LOW

Salad

Gloriously simple to make, this Croatian dish is packed with flavour. It is traditionally cooked in a large, shallow earthenware pot and served with finely shredded white cabbage, tossed in red wine vinegar, olive oil and lots of black pepper.

16 washed **small potatoes**

4 small skinless **chicken portions**

4 small **pork chops**

4 small **lamb chops**

10 ml/2 tsp **chopped garlic** from a jar, or 2 **garlic cloves**, chopped

2 large sprigs of **rosemary**

1 large **bay leaf**

250 ml/8 fl oz/1 cup boiling **chicken stock**

Salt and freshly ground black pepper

45 ml/3 tbsp chopped fresh **parsley**

1   Arrange the potatoes in the base of the crock pot and place the meat on top. Add the garlic, rosemary and bay leaf, pour the stock over and season well.

2   Cover and cook on High for 3–5 hours or Low for 6–10 hours until all the meat is meltingly tender.

3   Taste and re-season, if necessary, and sprinkle with the parsley.

Serving tip

• If you don't fancy the salad suggestion, serve with a green vegetable.

kidneys in devil sauce

4

3 hrs LOW

Rice and green beans

Chef's note

Offal dishes are not to everyone's taste, but this one is truly delicious. This used to be a favourite Victorian breakfast dish, but for those of us with a lesser constitution, it makes a delicious lunch or supper dish. The only tiny bit of preparation is snipping the kidneys into pieces – not that arduous. Although it takes only a few hours to cook (best on Low), you can also leave it longer.

A good handful of **frozen diced onion**, or 1 **fresh onion**, chopped

10 ml/2 tsp softened **butter**

350 g/12 oz packet of **frozen lambs' kidneys**, thawed, or 7 or 8 **fresh kidneys**

50 g/2 oz **unsmoked lardons** (diced bacon)

100 g/4 oz **fresh baby button** or **frozen sliced mushrooms**

5 ml/1 tsp **curry paste**

5 ml/1 tsp made **English mustard**

30 ml/2 tbsp **tomato purée** (paste)

15 ml/1 tbsp **light brown sugar**

15 ml/1 tbsp **Worcestershire sauce**

15 ml/1 tbsp **cornflour** (cornstarch)

15 ml/1 tbsp **water**

Salt and freshly ground black pepper

A few dried **chives** to garnish

1 Mix the onion with the butter in the crock pot.

2 Hold one kidney at a time over the pot and snip into chunks with scissors, discarding the white core. You don't have to be meticulous, just snip into three or four pieces, roughly round the core and throw the core away (but it doesn't matter if a little of the core is left on the kidney pieces). Add the lardons and mushrooms.

3 Mix together all the remaining ingredients except the chive garnish and pour over. Stir well to coat everything in the sauce.

4 Cover and cook on Low for 3 hours until the kidneys are tender and the sauce has thickened. Stir, taste and re-season if necessary.

5 Serve sprinkled with chives, with rice and green beans.

Cook's tips

• For brunch or a light lunch, serve these spooned over buttered wholegrain toast.

garlic & mint lamb

4-5

8-10hrs

LOW

Broccoli and redcurrant jelly (clear conserve)

Chef's note

Peas, mint and lamb have long been excellent companions and this is a simple but mouth-watering way to serve them together. Here, like many recipes in this book, the potatoes are also cooked in the pot, so all you have to cook at the end is some broccoli.

½ small lean **leg of lamb**, about 700 g/1½ lb

Salt and freshly ground black pepper

10 ml/2 tsp **chopped garlic** from a jar, or 2 **garlic cloves**, chopped

5 ml/1 tsp **dried mint**

450 g/1 lb washed **small potatoes**

250 ml/8 fl oz/1 cup boiling **lamb** or **chicken stock**

45 ml/3 tbsp **cornflour** (cornstarch)

45 ml/3 tbsp **water**

225 g/8 oz/2 cups **frozen peas**, thawed

1   Put the lamb in the crock pot and rub all over with salt, pepper and the garlic. Sprinkle with the mint. Put the potatoes all round and season them lightly with salt. Pour the boiling stock around.

2   Cover and cook on Low for 8–10 hours until everything is really tender.

3   Transfer the lamb to a carving dish and keep warm. Lift out the potatoes with a draining spoon and place in a dish. Keep warm.

4   Turn up the crock pot to High and spoon off any fat from the cooking liquid. Blend the cornflour with the water and stir in, then stir in the peas. Taste and re-season, if necessary. Cover and leave to cook while you carve the lamb into chunky pieces.

5   Put the lamb and potatoes in warm shallow bowls. Spoon the gravy over the lamb.

6   Serve with broccoli and redcurrant jelly.

Cook's tip
• You could stir a spoonful of redcurrant jelly into the sauce when you thicken it, if you like.

red-cooked lamb & peppers

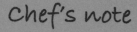

4

4 hrs HIGH
or **8** hrs LOW

Chinese egg noodles

2 good handfuls of **frozen sliced mixed (bell) peppers**, or 1 red and 1 green fresh **pepper**, sliced

700 g/1½ lb lean **diced lamb**

10 ml/2 tsp **chopped garlic** from a jar, or 1 large **garlic clove**, chopped

A good handful of **frozen diced onion**, or 4 **spring onions** (scallions), chopped

5 ml/1 tsp **root ginger** from a jar, or use freshly grated

5 ml/1 tsp **Chinese five-spice powder**

15 ml/1 tbsp **tomato purée** (paste)

15 ml/1 tbsp **cornflour** (cornstarch)

30 ml/2 tbsp **dry sherry**

75 ml/5 tbsp **soy sauce**

150 ml/¼ pt/⅔ cup boiling **lamb stock**

40 g/1½ oz/3 tbsp **light brown sugar**

1   Reserve a few slices of pepper for garnish. Put the remainder in the crock pot with the lamb, garlic and onion.

2   Mix together all the remaining ingredients and pour over. Stir well.

3   Cover and cook on High for 3–4 hours or Low for 6–8 hours until the lamb is tender and bathed in a rich sauce. Stir gently.

4   Serve spooned over noodles, garnished with the reserved pepper slices.

Serving tip

• You can also serve this with beansprouts tossed in a little sunflower oil, soy sauce and lemon juice.

pork, bacon & ham dishes

You can't beat British outdoor-reared pork for flavour and succulence – particularly when it is slow cooked. Here I've used all sorts of cuts of fresh and cured pork in a variety of ways to show you just how versatile it can be. Whether you like a taste of Asia – like my gently braised Sweet and Sour Pork with pineapple and mixed vegetables or Yellow Pork and Sweetcorn Curry – or prefer something more British like my Stuffing-topped Rack of Pork, you'll find an abundance of recipes for every occasion to tempt your taste buds.

Tips for great slow-cooked pork, bacon and ham

- Only use frozen meat that has been thoroughly defrosted.

- Choose the leanest pork or bacon you can find for slow cooking. Unlike grilling or roasting, you don't need the fat to keep it moist.

- You can use different liquids when cooking meat. Try replacing half the stock in any pork recipe with dry cider, for example.

- Remember that bacon can be salty, so avoid adding more salt until you have tasted the dish towards the end of cooking.

- To watch progress without lifting the lid – and losing heat – twist the lid so the moisture falls back into the crock pot and you can see through the glass.

sweet & sour pork

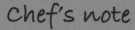
This is a firm family favourite – tender pork, juicy pineapple and colourful shredded vegetables, flavoured with soy sauce, ginger and tomato. Served over noodles or rice, it makes a perfect meal any day of the week.

3 hrs HIGH
or **6** hrs LOW

Egg noodles or rice and extra soy sauce (optional)

450 g/1 lb lean **diced pork**

300 g/11 oz/medium can of **pineapple pieces** in natural juice

90 ml/6 tbsp **soy sauce**

5 ml/1 tsp **chopped garlic** from a jar, or 1 **garlic clove**, chopped

15 ml/1 tbsp **tomato ketchup** (catsup)

10 ml/2 tsp **clear honey**

2.5 ml/½ tsp **ground ginger**

30 ml/2 tbsp **cornflour** (cornstarch)

300 g/11 oz fresh or frozen shredded **stir-fry vegetables with beansprouts**

1   Put everything except the stir-fry vegetables in the crock pot.

2   Cover and cook on High for 2 hours or Low for 4 hours.

3   Stir in the vegetables, cover and cook for a further 1 hour on High or 2 hours on Low.

4   Serve over noodles or rice with extra soy sauce to sprinkle over, if liked.

Cook's tip

• If you're going out, you can add the vegetables at the beginning but the result won't have the slight crunchy texture.

choucroute garni

Chef's note

You can buy this in street markets in many parts of France and it is rich and delicious. It really benefits from long, slow cooking so is the ideal dish for your slow cooker. Normally it has big slabs of meat that are cut up at the end. But for this lazy version, you don't even have to do that!

4

5 hrs HIGH or
10 hrs LOW

Potatoes and mustard

A good handful of **frozen diced onion**, or 1 **fresh onion**, chopped

15 ml/1 tbsp softened **butter**

700 g/1½ lb jar of **sauerkraut**, rinsed and drained

4 jumbo **frankfurters**

4 large **belly pork slices**, halved

100 g/4 oz **smoked lardons** (diced bacon)

1.5 ml/¼ tsp **ground cloves**

1 large **bay leaf**

120 ml/4 fl oz/½ cup dry **white wine**

120 ml/4 fl oz/½ cup boiling **chicken stock**

Salt and freshly ground black pepper

A little chopped fresh or frozen **parsley** to garnish

1   Mix the onion with the butter in the crock pot. Add the sauerkraut and spread out. Arrange all the meats over, add the cloves and tuck in the bay leaf.

2   Pour the wine and stock over and season well.

3   Cover and cook on High for 4–5 hours or Low for 8–10 hours until everything is tender and the meat is colouring slightly.

4   Discard the bay leaf and taste and re-season, if necessary. Sprinkle with parsley.

5   Serve with plain boiled potatoes and mustard.

Cook's tip
• For large appetites, add extra pork slices.

pork with coriander & wine

4

4 hrs HIGH
or 8 hrs LOW

Rice and a
mixed salad

The proper way to roughly crush coriander seed is in a mortar with a pestle; however, it's easy enough in a small bowl with the end of a rolling pin or a well-washed bottle. You could use half the quantity of the ground spice, if you can't be bothered to do a little bit of crushing (it only takes a minute or two), but it won't have the same glorious fragrance.

700 g / 1½ lb lean **diced pork**

200 ml/7 fl oz/scant 1 cup **red wine**

10 ml/2 tsp **tomato purée** (paste)

5 ml/1 tsp **clear honey**

Salt and freshly ground black pepper

10 ml/2 tsp **coriander seeds**, roughly crushed

2.5 ml/½ tsp **dried oregano**

1   Put all the ingredients in the crock pot and stir well. Cover and cook on High for 4 hours or Low for 8 hours.

2   Taste and re-season if necessary. Serve spooned over rice with a mixed salad.

Serving tip
• Top your mixed salad with olives and crumbled Feta cheese for an extra-special salad.

braised pork chops in tomato

4 hrs HIGH
or **8** hrs LOW

Pasta or potato gnocchi

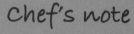

Chef's note

Pork chops can often be disappointingly dry and tough. Slow cooking them in a tomato and caper sauce with fragrant rosemary gives them a fabulous flavour and renders them tender and succulent.

45 ml/3 tbsp **plain (all-purpose) flour**

Salt and freshly ground black pepper

4 large **pork chops**

400 g/14 oz/large can of **chopped tomatoes**

150 ml/¼ pt/⅔ cup **red wine**

60 ml/4 tbsp **red wine vinegar**

75 ml/5 tbsp **water**

5 ml/1 tsp **caster (superfine) sugar**

5 ml/1 tsp **chopped garlic** from a jar, or 1 **garlic clove,** chopped

15 ml/1 tbsp **chopped pickled capers**

1.5 ml/¼ tsp **crushed dried chillies** (optional)

1 **bay leaf**

A sprig of fresh **rosemary**

1   Mix the flour with a little salt and pepper in the crock pot. Add the chops and turn to coat completely. Lift them out.

2   Add the tomatoes, wine, vinegar, water, sugar, garlic, capers and chillies, if using, to the crock pot. Stir well. Return the chops to the pot and push them well down into the mixture. Season again. Add the bay leaf and rosemary.

3   Cover and cook on High for 4 hours or Low for 8 hours until the chops are really tender.

4   Discard the bay leaf and rosemary, taste and re-season, if necessary.

5   Serve with pasta or potato gnocchi.

Serving tip

- Any pasta will go well, but I like a robust shape, like farfalle or conchiglie.

creamy paprika pork

Chef's note

This rich, creamy Hungarian dish is also good made with chicken or beef. Use sweet or hot paprika, whichever you prefer – I like the sweet one for this dish, but you may want something with a bit more bite.

4 hrs HIGH or 8 hrs LOW

Noodles and a green salad

15 ml/1 tbsp **paprika**

45 ml/3 tbsp **plain (all-purpose) flour**

700 g/1½ lb **diced pork**

15 ml/1 tbsp **sunflower oil**

A handful of **frozen diced onion**, or 1 **fresh onion**, chopped

300 ml/½ pt/1¼ cups boiling **chicken stock**

200 g/7 oz/1 small can of **pimientos** (sweet red peppers), drained and cut into strips

Salt and freshly ground black pepper

5 ml/1 tsp **caster (superfine) sugar**

150 ml/¼ pt/⅔ cup **soured (dairy sour) cream**

15 ml/1 tbsp chopped fresh **parsley** to garnish

1   Mix the paprika and flour, then toss the pork in the mixture and put in the crock pot.

2   Mix the oil, onions and pimientos and stir in.

3   Pour over the hot stock and season with a little salt and pepper and the sugar. Stir well.

4   Cover and cook on High for 3–4 hours or Low for 6–8 hours until the meat is really tender.

5   Stir in the soured cream, taste and re-season, if necessary. Garnish with the parsley.

6   Serve on a bed of noodles, with a green salad.

Serving tip
• If you like sauerkraut, try serving it hot, sprinkled with caraway seeds, instead of the green salad.

thai red pork curry

4

3 hrs HIGH
or **6** hrs LOW

Rice noodles

Chef's note

This curry is simplicity itself to prepare. You can substitute chicken for the pork, or if you prefer beef, cook for an extra hour on High or 2 hours on Low.

400 ml/14 oz/1 large can of **coconut milk**

30 ml/2 tbsp **Thai red curry paste**

2 fat **red chillies**, seeded, if preferred, and cut into thin strips

5 ml/1 tsp **palm** or **light brown sugar**

2.5 ml/½ tsp **salt**

450 g/1 lb **diced pork**

30 ml/2 tbsp chopped fresh **coriander** (cilantro)

1   Heat the coconut milk in a pan with the curry paste, chillies, sugar and salt until boiling.

2   Spread out the pork in the crock pot and pour the sauce over.

3   Cover and cook on High for 3 hours or Low for 6 hours until really tender.

4   Serve spooned over rice noodles, sprinkled with the coriander.

Cook's tip

• This is also delicious with two large handfuls of large raw peeled prawns thrown in for the last 30 minutes' cooking until they have just turned pink. If using frozen prawns, make sure they are thawed and well drained before adding them to the crock pot.

rich liver pâté & apple brandy

6-8

2 hrs HIGH
or **4** hrs LOW

Hot toast

You can, of course, use ordinary brandy, but I just love Calvados from Normandy and use it in my cooking whenever I can. Adding a few dried apple rings offsets the richness of the liver and adds a subtle sweetness, but you can omit them if you don't have any.

100 g/4 oz/½ cup **butter**

450 g/1 lb sliced **pigs' liver**

6 rindless **streaky bacon** rashers (slices)

A good handful of **frozen diced onion**, or 1 **fresh onion**, chopped

5 ml/1 tsp **chopped garlic** from a jar, or 1 **garlic clove**, chopped

8 dried **apple rings**

120 ml/4 fl oz/½ cup **water**

30 ml/2 tbsp **Calvados**

2.5 ml/½ tsp **dried mixed herbs**

Salt and freshly ground black pepper

1   Put 50 g/2 oz/¼ cup of the butter in the crock pot with all the remaining ingredients, seasoning well.

2   Cover and cook on High for 2 hours or Low for 4 hours until cooked through.

3   Purée in a blender or food processor. Taste and re-season, if necessary, then turn into an attractive serving dish, level the surface and leave to cool.

4   Melt the remaining butter and pour over the surface in a thin layer. Chill until firm.

5   Serve with hot toast.

Serving tip
• This pâté is also good served with Melba toast.

pork & bean hotpot

Chef's note

Pork and beans are a popular combination. Here I've used haricot beans with diced pork and teamed them with mixed root vegetables, tomatoes and herbs for a very simple but tasty dish.

4

4 hrs HIGH
or **8** hrs LOW

Crusty bread

350 g/12 oz lean **diced pork**

225 g/8 oz frozen **casserole vegetables with celery**

2 x 400 g/14 oz/large cans of **haricot (navy) beans**, drained

400 g/14 oz/1 large can of **chopped tomatoes**

15 ml/1 tbsp **golden (light corn) syrup**

2.5 ml/½ tsp **dried chives**

2.5 ml/½ tsp **dried sage**

Salt and freshly ground black pepper

A few extra **dried chives** to garnish

1   Mix together all the ingredients except the chive garnish in the crock pot.

2   Cover and cook on High for 4 hours or Low for 8 hours until everything is meltingly tender and bathed in sauce.

3   Taste and re-season, if necessary. Spoon into warm bowls and sprinkle with chives.

4   Serve with crusty bread.

Cook's tip
- You can use other beans if you prefer, such as cannellini or black-eyed.

yellow pork & sweetcorn curry

4-6

4 hrs HIGH
or **8** hrs LOW

Rice noodles

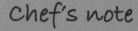

Chef's note

This is not an authentic Thai curry, just a creation of mine. I love the flavour of the yellow curry paste with pork. It is very simple to throw together, but the rich, fragrant end result will taste as if you've slaved over a hot stove for hours!

30 ml/2 tbsp **Thai yellow curry paste**

30 ml/2 tbsp **dried onion flakes**

5 ml/1 tsp **chopped garlic** from a jar, or 1 **garlic clove**, chopped

10 ml/2 tsp **grated galangal** or **root ginger** from a jar

5 ml/1 tsp **lemon grass** from a jar (optional)

10 ml/2 tsp **Thai fish sauce** (nam pla)

15 ml/1 tbsp **light brown sugar**

400 ml/14 oz/large can of **coconut milk**

175 g/6 oz/1½ cups **frozen sweetcorn**

700 g/1½ lb **diced pork**

Salt and freshly ground black pepper

A few torn fresh **coriander (cilantro) leaves** to garnish

1   Mix together everything except the pork, seasoning and coriander garnish in the crock pot until well blended. Stir in the pork and season lightly.

2   Cover and cook on High for 4 hours or Low for 8 hours until really tender.

3   Taste and re-season, if necessary, and sprinkle with torn coriander leaves.

4   Serve spooned over rice noodles.

Serving tip

• You might also like to try this served with jasmine rice.

ribs with a tickle of tabasco sauce

4 hrs HIGH or 8 hrs LOW

Coleslaw and salad

Chef's note

Slow cooking the ribs makes them so meltingly tender that the meat simply falls off the bones when you eat them. Add as much Tabasco sauce as you dare, or do as I do and add just a few drops to cook, then extra when nibbling! Lining the pot prevents the ribs burning and makes cleaning easier. Use a large crock pot for these.

15 ml/1 tbsp **sunflower oil**

5 ml/1 tsp **sesame oil**

10 ml/2 tsp **root ginger** from a jar, or use freshly grated

45 ml/3 tbsp **clear honey**

10 ml/2 tsp **Chinese five-spice powder**

10 ml/2 tsp **chopped garlic** from a jar, or 1 large **garlic clove**, chopped

A few drops of **Tabasco sauce**

75 ml/5 tbsp **soy sauce**

900 g/2 lb **Chinese short spare ribs**

1 Mix together everything except the ribs in a large dish. Add the ribs and turn to coat completely.

2 Line the crock pot with non-stick baking parchment, making sure it comes up the sides of the pot. Arrange the ribs in the pot, bone-sides up. Spoon over the remaining marinade.

3 Cover and cook on High for 4 hours or Low for 8 hours until meltingly tender, turning and rearranging once during cooking.

4 Turn the ribs over in the cooking juices one last time, then lift out of the pot with tongs and serve hot with coleslaw and salad.

Serving tip

• Serve with a finger bowl and loads of paper napkins.

stuffing-topped rack of pork

4-6

3 hrs HIGH or **6** hrs LOW

New potatoes and a green vegetable

This delicious pot roast is perfect for Sunday lunch or dinner. You can try it with a lean belly pork joint, too, but make sure the rind has been removed before you put the stuffing on.

½ x 130 g/4½ oz packet of **sage, onion and garlic stuffing mix**

175 ml/6 fl oz/¾ cup boiling **water**

1 **egg**, beaten

Salt and freshly ground black pepper

1 skinless **bone-in pork loin** with 6 chops

225 g/8 oz **frozen carrots**

300 ml/½ pt /1¼ cups boiling **pork** or **beef stock**

15 ml/1 tbsp **brandy** (optional)

30 ml/2 tbsp **cornflour** (cornstarch)

30 ml/2 tbsp cold **water**

1   Make up the stuffing mix with the boiling water, following the instructions on the packet, then stir in the beaten egg.

2   Season the pork and put in the crock pot, skinned-side up. Press the stuffing all over the skinned side of the pork. Arrange the carrots around, pour the stock around and add the brandy, if using.

3   Cover and cook on High for 3 hours or Low for 6 hours until tender.

4   Carefully lift the pork out of the crock pot and put on a carving dish. Keep warm. Lift out the carrots with a draining spoon and keep warm.

5   Blend the cornflour with the cold water and stir into the juices in the crock pot. Turn the pot to High, if on Low. Cover and leave while you dish up.

6   Cut the meat into chops, keeping the stuffing pressed on the surface.

7   Serve with the carrots, new potatoes, a green vegetable and the gravy.

Cook's tip

• If you like apple sauce with your pork, buy a jar of it instead of making your own, to save even more effort.

gammon with apple & carrots

4-6

4 hrs HIGH
or **8** hrs LOW

Green beans,
mustard and
redcurrant jelly
(clear conserve)

Chef's note

When you boil gammon in a pot, you can cook vegetables with it but there's lots of steam and loads of liquid; if you roast it in the oven, it can be dry and you have to cook the vegetables separately. In the slow cooker you get the best of both worlds – succulent, tender gammon and veggies – and no steam in your kitchen!

900 g/2 lb **gammon joint**, soaked, if necessary, according to the directions on the packet

450 g/1 lb washed **baby potatoes**

225 g/8 oz fresh or frozen **baby carrots**

25 g/1 oz **dried apple rings**

250 ml/8 fl oz/1 cup **medium-sweet cider**

150 ml/¼ pt/⅔ cup boiling **water**

1 **bay leaf**

45 ml/3 tbsp **cornflour** (cornstarch)

45 ml/3 tbsp cold **water**

Opposite: Gammon with Apple and Carrots (see above)

1   Put the meat in the crock pot, skin-side up. Arrange the potatoes, carrots and apple rings around the joint. Pour the cider and water around and add the bay leaf.

2   Cover and cook on High for 4 hours or Low for 8 hours.

3   Carefully lift the gammon out of the pot and transfer to a warm carving dish. Remove the apple rings, potatoes and carrots with a draining spoon and keep warm.

4   Turn the pot up to High, if on Low. Blend the cornflour with the water and stir into the cooking juices. Taste and re-season, if necessary. Cover and leave to thicken while you carve the meat.

5   Cut or pull off all the rind (it should come away easily). Cut the meat into fairly thick slices, then put on plates with the potatoes, carrots and apples. Spoon some of the thickened cooking juices over the meat and pour the remainder into a gravy boat.

6   Serve with green beans, the remaining thickened cooking juices, mustard and redcurrant jelly.

Serving tip
• I like to try different mustards. Many are sweeter than the traditional English mustard, so if you find that too harsh, give a milder one a try.

Opposite: American-style Meatloaf (see pages 100–101)

pork with grilled peppers

4

4 hrs HIGH
or 8 hrs LOW

Egg noodles

700 g/1½ lb lean **diced pork**

45 ml/3 tbsp **plain (all-purpose) flour**

Salt and freshly ground black pepper

15 ml/1 tbsp **paprika**

30 ml/2 tbsp **dried onion flakes**

2 good handfuls of **frozen grilled (broiled) (bell) peppers**

5 ml/1 tsp **caster (superfine) sugar**

300 ml/½ pt/1¼ cups boiling **chicken stock**

150 ml/¼ pt/⅔ cup **crème fraîche**

A little chopped fresh or frozen **parsley** to garnish

1   Mix together everything except the stock, crème fraîche and parsley garnish in the crock pot.

2   Stir in the stock, cover and cook on High for 3–4 hours or Low for 6–8 hours until the pork is tender and the sauce is thick.

3   Stir in the crème fraîche and season to taste again. Sprinkle with parsley.

4   Serve with egg noodles.

Cook's tip
• Frozen peppers make a great standby, as you can use them straight from the freezer.

fish dishes

Fish doesn't take long to cook conventionally but it is all too easy to overcook it, making it dry and unpalatable. By using a slow cooker, nearly always set to Low, you can guarantee moist, tender results. You can't leave it all day, as you would meat or poultry, but it will sit happily for an hour or two without needing your attention. So, as the recipes are so quick to put together, you can come home, throw the ingredients into the pot and then go and do something else while it cooks.

Do experiment with different fish; they all cook in the same length of time, so you can interchange a similar type according to what's the best buy at your local fishmonger. Most can be cooked from frozen unless I state otherwise in the recipe.

Tips for great slow-cooked fish

- Fish dishes are usually best cooked on Low.

- Most fish dishes will cook in 1–2 hours maximum.

- Most fish can be cooked from frozen.

- Unlike casseroles or other meat dishes, fish should not be left too long once it has cooked, as it is much more delicate and will tend to dry out if left too long.

- Thin pieces of fish can be rolled before being cooked in the slow cooker.

- A dash of white wine can be added to most fish recipes.

- Don't remove the lid while the fish is cooking – you'll lose heat and moisture. Twist it to shake off the moisture so you can see through.

poached salmon & prawns

4

2 hrs LOW

New potatoes and peas

4 frozen **salmon steaks**

Salt and freshly ground black pepper

60 ml/4 tbsp **mayonnaise**

100 g/4 oz frozen cooked peeled **prawns** (shrimp)

2.5 ml/½ tsp **dried dill** (dill weed)

Wedges of **lemon** to garnish

Chef's note

This dish couldn't be simpler, but it looks and tastes delicious. You use the seafood from frozen so you don't even have to remember to get it out of the freezer in advance. I would suggest the simple accompaniments of new potatoes and peas – and perhaps a little extra mayonnaise to serve on the side.

1   Pour enough boiling water in the crock pot to just cover the base – no more. Put the salmon in the pot and season lightly.

2   Mix the mayonnaise with the prawns, the dill and a little seasoning. Pile on top of the salmon steaks.

3   Cover and cook on Low for 1–2 hours (depending on the thickness of the fish) until it is cooked through.

4   Transfer to warm plates, garnish with wedges of lemon and serve straight away.

5   Accompany with new potatoes and peas.

Serving tip
• Salmon is so versatile, you could serve this with almost any accompaniments.

cod steaks with pesto

Chef's note

I've used traditional green basil pesto here, though you could use coriander, rocket or even the red tomato pesto, if you prefer. The jars are really good and easily available in any supermarket.

4

2 hrs
LOW

A mixed salad

25 g/1 oz/2 tbsp unsalted (sweet) **butter**

60 ml/4 tbsp **dry white wine**

60 ml/4 tbsp boiling **water**

Salt and freshly ground black pepper

4 frozen **cod steaks**

30 ml/2 tbsp **basil pesto** from a jar

½ **lemon**, sliced

8 **vermicelli 'nests'** (or according to appetite)

30 ml/2 tbsp freshly grated **Parmesan cheese**, plus extra to garnish

Wedges of **lemon** and a few torn fresh **basil leaves** to garnish

1   Drop the butter in flakes into the crock pot. Add the wine and boiling water, cover and cook on High while you prepare the fish.

2   Season the cod steaks and spread with the pesto. Put the lemon slices in the butter and wine mixture and lay the fish in the pot.

3   Cover and cook on Low for 2 hours until the fillets are cooked through.

4   Meanwhile, cook the vermicelli according to the packet directions. Drain.

5   When the fish is cooked, carefully lift it out of the pot with a fish slice, place on a platter and keep warm. Discard the lemon slices. Add the vermicelli to the juices in the pot and toss well. Sprinkle in the Parmesan and toss again.

6   Pile the pasta on to warm plates and top with the fish. Garnish with a sprinkling of Parmesan, wedges of lemon and torn basil leaves.

7   Serve with a mixed salad.

Serving tip

• I've chosen vermicelli for this recipe because it is so quick to cook, but try any long-stranded pasta such as spaghetti or linguine.

smoked salmon tart

4

2 hrs
HIGH

A mixed salad

1 ready-baked **pastry case** (pie shell)

100 g/4 oz ready-washed fresh **spinach**

Salt and freshly ground black pepper

120 g/4½ oz packet of **smoked salmon trimmings**

120 ml/4 fl oz/½ cup **crème fraîche**

2.5 ml/½ tsp dried **dill** (dill weed)

1 Put the pastry case in its foil in the crock pot. Squeeze the spinach in your hands to crush it slightly and pack it into the pastry case (it will be quite a pile). Season with a little salt and lots of pepper.

2 Crumble the salmon over to separate it as much as possible (it won't cover the spinach completely). Spoon the crème fraîche over and sprinkle with the dill. You should have patches of cream, patches of green and patches of pink.

3 Cover and cook on High for 2 hours until the spinach is cooked and wilted.

4 Serve warm or cold with a mixed salad.

Serving tip
• Try using a drained can of tuna instead of smoked salmon and scatter a few capers over for added piquancy.

Cook's tip
• For a change, you could use parsley instead of dill.

smoked haddock florentine

4

2 hrs LOW

Wholemeal toast and butter

450 g/1 lb ready-washed fresh or thawed frozen leaf **spinach**

1.5 ml/¼ tsp **ground nutmeg**

4 fresh or frozen **smoked haddock fillets**, about 150 g/5 oz each

200 ml/7 fl oz/scant 1 cup **crème fraîche**

10 ml/2 tsp **cornflour** (cornstarch)

100 g/4 oz/1 cup ready-grated **Cheddar cheese**

Salt and freshly ground black pepper

1   Squeeze fresh spinach, if using, to compact it a bit or the thawed spinach to remove as much moisture as possible. Spread out in a shallow flameproof dish that will just fit in a large crock pot. Sprinkle with the nutmeg.

2   Lay the fish on top, putting the fillets head to tail so they fit the space in an even layer.

3   Mix the crème fraîche with the cornflour and cheese. Season to taste with salt and pepper, then spoon over the fish. Place the dish in the crock pot and pour round enough boiling water to come half-way up the sides of the dish.

4   Cover and cook on Low for 2 hours until the sauce is set and the fish is cooked through.

5   Preheat the grill (broiler), transfer the dish to the grill and quickly brown the surface for about 5 minutes.

6   Serve hot with wholemeal toast and butter.

Serving tip
• This dish also goes well with nutty brown rice.

lemon sole in garlic butter

4

2 hrs
LOW

Rice and peas,
mixed together

Chef's note

Lemon sole is a delicate fish that work really well in the slow cooker. Here it is gently cooked in a savoury butter – simple but effective and much less prone to overcooking than when using a frying pan or the grill.

4 small whole **lemon sole**

Salt and freshly ground black pepper

50 g/2 oz/¼ cup **butter**, cut into small pieces

60 ml/4 tbsp **olive oil**

5 ml/1 tsp **chopped garlic** from a jar, or 1 **garlic clove**, chopped

30 ml/2 tbsp chopped fresh or frozen **parsley**

15 ml/1 tbsp chopped fresh **tarragon**, or 2.5 ml/½ tsp dried

15 ml/1 tbsp **lime juice**

15 ml/1 tbsp **pickled capers**, rinsed

1   Lightly season the fish with salt and pepper. Place in the crock pot (they will have to overlap slightly).

2   Dot with the butter and drizzle with the oil. Make sure each fish is coated in oil where they overlap just to make completely sure they don't stick together. Add all the remaining ingredients.

3   Cover and cook on Low for 2 hours until the fish is cooked through.

4   Taste and re-season the fish, if necessary. Carefully transfer the fish and caper butter mixture to warm plates.

5   Serve with rice mixed with peas.

Cook's tip

• Take care not to over-season, or you will lose the delicate flavour of the fish.

seafood rigatoni in saffron sauce

I first had a version of this, shells and all, in Spain about ten years ago. This is my simple, quick adaptation for the slow cooker and what it lacks in spectacular appearance, it makes up for on taste. Unlike most fish dishes, this is best cooked on High. I like to serve it while the pasta still has a little texture and there is plenty of lovely saffron-favoured sauce to mop up with some ciabatta bread.

4

1 ½ hrs HIGH

A mixed salad

350 g/12 oz **rigatoni**

30 ml/2 tbsp **olive oil**

5 ml/1 tsp **chopped garlic** from a jar, or 1 **garlic clove**, chopped

5 ml/1 tsp **dried chives**

2.5 ml/½ tsp **saffron strands**

400 g/14 oz **frozen raw seafood cocktail**

2 good handfuls of **frozen mixed (bell) peppers**

1 litre/1¾ pts/4¼ cups boiling **fish** or **chicken stock**

Salt and freshly ground black pepper

A little chopped fresh or frozen **parsley** to garnish

Opposite: Poached Salmon with Prawns (see pages 166–7)

1   Toss the pasta in the oil in the crock pot, then mix in all the remaining ingredients.

2   Cover and cook on High for 1½ hours, stirring once half-way through cooking and again at the end of cooking to ensure all the pasta is bathed in sauce.

3   Best served straight away but, if not quite ready to eat, you can turn the cooker off and leave it a short while. It will absorb more of the liquid and the pasta will become quite soft.

4   Serve with a mixed salad.

Serving tip

• This is a lovely dish that's great hot, warm or even cold.

Opposite: Bean and Vegetable Braise (see pages 188–9)

mackerel with chillies & olives

4

2 hrs LOW

Rice

Chef's note

You can make this dish using other whole fish, such as red snapper or herring. It's also good with fresh sardines, but you'll need two or three per person (depending on size).

4 small cleaned **mackerel**

Salt and freshly ground black pepper

400 g/14 oz/1 large can of **chopped tomatoes**

60 ml/4 tbsp **dry white wine**

30 ml/2 tbsp **sun-dried** (or ordinary) **tomato purée** (paste)

2.5 ml/½ tsp crushed **dried chillies**

15 ml/1 tbsp **dried chives**, plus a few extra to garnish

12 green or black **olives** (try those flavoured with garlic and herbs)

1   Rinse the mackerel inside and out and pat dry on kitchen paper (paper towels). Make a few slashes on each side of them and lay them in the crock pot. Season with salt and pepper.

2   Mix the chopped tomatoes with the wine, tomato purée, chillies and chives. Pour over the fish, then scatter with the olives.

3   Cover and cook on Low for 2 hours or until the fish is cooked through.

4   Taste and re-season, if necessary. Carefully lift the fish out of the pot and transfer to a bed of rice on warm plates. Spoon the sauce over and sprinkle with a few dried chives.

Cook's tip
• This is equally delicious made with chicken; simply substitute skinless chicken breasts for the mackerel and cook for 3 hours on High or 6 hours on Low.

squid in garlic oil with peppers

4-6

2 hrs LOW

Crusty bread and a green salad

Chef's note

Squid rings are readily available at every supermarket fish counter. They can be rubbery when fried, but when gently cooked in oil in your slow cooker they become tender and delicious. Don't buy the frozen ones in batter or breadcrumbs – they are not right for this dish.

900 g/2 lb prepared **squid rings**

2 good handfuls of **frozen sliced mixed (bell) peppers**, or 1 red and 1 green **pepper**, sliced

A good handful of **frozen diced onion**, or 1 **fresh onion**, chopped

10 ml/2 tsp **chopped garlic** from a jar, or 2 **garlic cloves**, chopped

90 ml/6 tbsp **olive oil**

2.5 ml/½ tsp **crushed dried chillies**

30 ml/2 tbsp **lemon juice**

2.5 ml/½ tsp **dried thyme**

Salt and freshly ground black pepper

30 ml/2 tbsp chopped fresh or frozen **parsley**

Wedges of **lemon** to garnish

1   Put all the ingredients except the parsley and lemon wedges for garnishing in the crock pot and toss well.

2   Cover and cook on Low for 2 hours until the squid is tender.

3   Switch off the slow cooker, taste and re-season, if necessary. Gently stir in the parsley. Re-cover and leave to stand for 5 minutes to allow the flavours to develop.

4   Spoon into bowls, and garnish with wedges of lemon.

5   Serve with crusty bread and a green salad.

Serving tip
• If you think you don't like squid, this recipe will be a pleasant surprise!

tuna steaks with harissa

4

2 hrs LOW

Warm pitta bread and a green salad

Chef's note

Harissa paste is a rich, red, fiery paste used extensively in North African cookery. I love it with fish, poultry and meat. If you use frozen tuna, you may find the juices set a little around them as they cook. Simply lift up the fish and stir them gently into the cooked bean mixture before serving.

A good handful of **frozen diced onion**, or 1 **fresh onion**, chopped

5 ml/1 tsp **chopped garlic** from a jar, or 1 **garlic clove**, chopped

400 g/14 oz/1 large can of **chopped tomatoes**

30 ml/2 tbsp **tomato purée** (paste)

A good pinch of **caster (superfine) sugar**

225 g/8 oz frozen **butternut squash**

2 x 400 g/14 oz/large cans of **haricot (navy)** or **cannellini beans**, drained

5 ml/1 tsp **dried oregano**

4 fresh or frozen **tuna steaks**

30 ml/2 tbsp **harissa paste**

Salt and freshly ground black pepper

1   Put the onion, garlic, tomatoes, tomato purée, sugar, squash, beans and oregano in the crock pot. Stir well.

2   Pat the fish dry with kitchen paper (paper towels). Smear the steaks with the harissa paste and place on top of the bean mixture. Season lightly.

3   Cover and cook on Low for 2 hours until the fish and squash are tender.

4   Break up the squash a bit, if the chunks are large.

5   Serve the dish straight from the pot with warm pitta breads and a green salad.

Serving tip
• If you warm pitta bread in the microwave for a few seconds, it will be softer and easier to handle. Alternatively, toast them briefly.

barley & kipper kedgeree

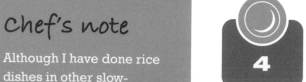  

4

1 hr HIGH
or **2** hrs LOW

Complete meal in itself

225 g/8 oz/generous 1 cup **pearl barley**

30 ml/2 tbsp **dried onion flakes**

5 ml/1 tsp **ground turmeric**

Salt and freshly ground black pepper

600 ml/1 pt/2½ cups boiling **fish, vegetable** or **chicken stock**

220 g/8 oz packet of **cook-in-the-bag kippers**

2 **eggs**, scrubbed under cold water

100 g/4 oz/1 cup **frozen peas**, thawed

60 ml/4 tbsp **single (light) cream**

30 ml/2 tbsp chopped fresh or frozen **parsley**

1 Mix the barley with the onion, turmeric and some salt and pepper in the crock pot. Pour the boiling stock over and stir.

2 Open the packet of kippers, separate them and lay them in the pot, skin-sides up, adding the pat of butter, if there is one. Wrap the eggs in greaseproof (waxed) paper, if you prefer, and add to the pot. This just makes them less slippery when you peel them.

3 Cover and cook on High for 1 hour or Low for 2 hours until the barley is tender and has absorbed most of the liquid.

4 Remove the eggs. Scrape the skin off the fish, then gently break up the flesh.

5 Lightly stir the peas and cream into the pot. Taste and re-season, if necessary. Cover and leave to heat through while you shell the eggs and cut them into wedges.

6 Spoon the kedgeree on to warm plates and top with the eggs. Garnish with the parsley and serve.

Serving tips

- If you're really hungry, serve with thin slices of buttered brown bread.
- Try serving it with 3–4 small smoked mackerel or trout fillets, too.

pulse-based dishes

Pulses are packed with vegetable protein so are ideal for vegetarians, but they are good for us all as they provide fibre, carbohydrates and some vitamins and minerals, too.

You can use your slow cooker to cook soaked dried beans from scratch. They take about 3 hours on High or 6 hours on Low, but must first be boiled for 10 minutes in water to remove toxins.

I've usually opted for canned beans in this no-effort book; I find them preferable to frozen ones as they have a better texture in the finished dish and are cheaper. I've called for specific beans for specific dishes, but experiment yourself to find the ones with the flavour, texture and colour you like best.

pulse-based dishes

Tips for great slow-cooked pulses

- There's such a variety of canned pulses available that you can really ring the changes with your choice for each recipe.

- I've used canned pulses for convenience, but you may want to cook your own if you use them regularly, or you could use frozen.

- If cooking your own beans, allow 100 g/4 oz/⅔ cup per 400 g/ 14 oz/large can called for in the recipe.

- Most canned beans don't need rinsing before adding to the pot, but flageolet beans are best tipped into a colander and washed under the cold tap.

- Think about colour when making your choice – a pale sauce might benefit from a dash of colour rather than a white bean.

- Can sizes vary slightly but that won't make any difference to the recipes.

bean & vegetable braise

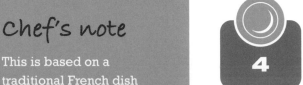  

4

8 hrs LOW

French bread and a green salad

Chef's note

This is based on a traditional French dish called cassoulet and usually takes quite a time to prepare. This slow-cooker version is moister than the real thing and everything is simply thrown into the pot and left to cook very slowly. It is rich and delicious and makes a wonderfully easy, hearty meal served with plenty of French bread.

225 g/8 oz **frozen casserole vegetables**

A good handful of **frozen diced onion** (or one **fresh onion**, chopped)

10 ml/2 tsp **chopped garlic** from a jar, or 1 large **garlic clove**, chopped

2 x 400g/14 oz/large cans of **haricot (navy) beans**, drained

2 x 400 g/14 oz/large cans of **chick peas (garbanzos)**

150 ml/¼ pt/⅔ cup boiling **chicken stock**

15 ml/1 tbsp **golden (light corn) syrup**

5 ml/1 tsp **Dijon mustard**

1 **bouquet garni sachet**

Salt and freshly ground black pepper

4 slices of **belly pork**

4 **chicken legs**

8 **pork chipolata sausages**

About 10 ml/2 tsp **soy sauce**

15 ml/1 tbsp **olive oil**

A few **dried chives** to garnish

1   Put the vegetables, onion and garlic in the crock pot. Add the drained beans, stock, syrup, mustard and bouquet garni. Season well and stir gently.

2   Lay all the meat on top of the vegetable mixture and brush with the soy sauce.

3   Cover and cook on Low for 6–8 hours until everything is tender and succulent. Quickly brush the meat again with soy sauce half-way through cooking, if liked, for a browner finish (but this isn't essential).

4   Taste and re-season, if necessary. Discard the bouquet garni.

5   Drizzle with the olive oil and a sprinkling of dried chives, and serve with French bread and a green salad.

Serving tip

• This casserole is so substantial, you might not need any accompaniments.

chick pea & vegetable tagine

4

3 hrs HIGH
or **6** hrs LOW

Mediterranean flat breads and a salad

chef's note

This Middle Eastern-style casserole is not only rich and tasty, but is also highly nutritious, packed full of vegetables, fruits and pulses. I like to serve it just with some Mediterranean flat breads and a salad, but you could serve rice or couscous, if you like.

2 x 400 g/14 oz/large cans of **chick peas** (garbanzos)

5 ml/1 tsp **chopped garlic** from a jar, or 1 **garlic clove**, chopped

225 g/8 oz **frozen casserole vegetables with celery**

5 ml/1 tsp **ground cumin**

5 ml/1 tsp **ground cinnamon**

100 g/4 oz whole **fresh baby button mushrooms** or **frozen sliced mushrooms**

400 g/14 oz/large can of **chopped tomatoes**

8 **ready-to-eat prunes**, halved, if preferred

30 ml/2 tbsp **tomato purée** (paste)

1 **bay leaf**

Salt and freshly ground black pepper

10 ml/2 tsp chopped fresh or frozen **coriander** (cilantro)

15 ml/1 tbsp **olive oil**

1   Drain one of the cans of chick peas and empty them into the crock pot. Add the contents of the second can, including the liquid.   Add all the remaining ingredients except the coriander and oil, and season well.

2   Cover and cook on High for 2–3 hours or Low for 4–6 hours until the vegetables are tender and everything is bathed in a rich sauce.

3   Discard the bay leaf, gently stir in the coriander, taste and re-season, if necessary. Spoon into bowls, trickle the olive oil over and serve hot.

4   Accompany with Mediterranean flat breads and a salad.

Serving tip
• Use a large handful of raisins instead of prunes if you prefer.

pulse-based dishes

chilli bean & vegetable stew

4

2 hrs HIGH
or **4** hrs LOW

Grated cheese

Chef's note

Hot, spicy and warming, this dish makes a great meal with crusty bread, served in crispy tacos or piled on a bed of fluffy rice. Use a cheese with a good strong flavour. Use less chilli if you don't like fire!

2 x 400 g/14 oz/large cans of **red kidney beans**, drained

A good handful of **frozen diced onion**, or 1 **fresh onion**, chopped

5 ml/1 tsp **chopped garlic** from a jar, or 1 **garlic clove**, chopped

5–10 ml/1–2 tsp **crushed dried chillies**

5 ml/1 tsp **ground cumin**

2.5 ml/½ tsp **ground cinnamon**

15 ml/1 tbsp **paprika**

450 ml/¾ pt/2 cups **passata** (sieved tomatoes)

15 ml/1 tbsp **tomato purée** (paste)

1 **bay leaf**

5 ml/1 tsp **dried oregano**

450 g/1 lb **frozen country mixed vegetables** (any of the chunky ones, not small dice)

Salt and freshly ground black pepper

1   Put all the ingredients in the crock pot, seasoning to taste. Stir well.

2   Cover and cook on High for 2 hours or Low for 4 hours until everything is tender and bathed in sauce.

3   Serve sprinkled with lots of grated cheese.

Serving tip

- I like to add a dollop of soured (dairy sour) cream as well as the grated cheese, but it would also be good topped with guacamole (bought or home-made).

potato, pea & lentil curry

Chef's note

You can vary the flavour of this by using different curry pastes. I've simply called for mild or medium but you could use a jalfrezi, Madras or korma paste for this. The resulting dish should not be wet, just all the ingredients coated in the sauce.

4

3 hrs HIGH
or **6** hrs LOW

Naan bread and mango chutney

A good handful of **frozen diced onion**, or 1 **fresh onion**, chopped

5 ml/1 tsp **chopped garlic** from a jar, or 1 **garlic clove**, chopped

12 washed **baby potatoes**, halved

30 ml/2 tbsp mild or medium **curry paste**

2 x 425 g/15 oz/1 large can of **green** or **brown lentils**, drained

225 g/8 oz/2 cups **frozen peas**

150 ml/¼ pt/⅔ cup **Greek-style strained yoghurt**

75 ml/5 tbsp boiling **water**

Salt and freshly ground black pepper

30 ml/2 tbsp **desiccated (shredded) coconut**

15 ml/1 tbsp chopped fresh or frozen **coriander** (cilantro)

1 Mix together all the ingredients except the coriander in the crock pot.

2 Cover and cook on High for 2–3 hours or Low for 4–6 hours until everything is tender and just bathed in sauce. Add a tablespoonful or two more of boiling water if the curry seems a little dry.

3 Stir in the coriander, taste and add more salt and pepper, if necessary.

4 Serve hot with naan bread and mango chutney.

Serving tip
• You might like to serve a selection of Indian pickles – there's loads of choice in the supermarkets.

chick peas, bacon & chorizo

4 hrs HIGH
or 8 hrs LOW

Multigrain rolls
and unsalted
butter

Chef's note

I like to serve warm multigrain rolls and unsalted butter with this satisfying stew. You can, of course, cut up your own chorizo sausage. Choose sweet or hot according to taste but avoid the thinly sliced packs sold for salads as they don't cook well.

2 x 400 g/14 oz/large cans of **chick peas** (garbanzos)

A good handful of **frozen diced onion**, or 1 **fresh onion**, chopped

2.5 ml/½ tsp **chopped garlic** from a jar, or 1 small **garlic clove**, chopped

150 g/5 oz diced **pancetta**

100 g/4 oz ready-diced or thickly sliced **tapas chorizo**

400 g/14 oz/large can of **chopped tomatoes**

30 ml/2 tbsp **tomato purée** (paste)

2.5 ml/½ tsp **pimentón** (smoked paprika)

225 g/8 oz **frozen mixed vegetables**

Salt and freshly ground black pepper

1 **bay leaf**

A few **dried chives** to garnish

1   Drain one of the cans of beans and empty them into the crock pot. Add the contents of the second can, including the liquid.

2   Stir in all the remaining ingredients except the chives for garnishing. Season lightly.

3   Cover and cook on High for 4 hours or Low for 8 hours until everything is soft and bathed in a rich sauce.

4   Taste, re-season, if necessary and discard the bay leaf. Ladle into warm bowls and sprinkle with a few dried chives.

5   Serve with multigrain rolls and unsalted (sweet) butter.

Serving tip

- You may prefer some French bread or even some rolled-up warm flour tortillas to accompany this dish.

flageolet & butternut curry

4

2 hrs HIGH
or **4** hrs LOW

**Complete meal
in itself**

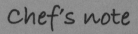
This is colourful and light and makes a really tasty meal. All you have to do is shell the eggs before serving. It is also nice served with soft poached eggs cooked separately just before serving instead of the hard-boiled ones, but that does mean a little more work!

4 **eggs**

30 ml/2 tbsp **olive oil**

30 ml/2 tbsp **dried onion flakes**

5 ml/1 tsp **chopped garlic** from a jar, or 1 **garlic clove**, chopped

5 ml/1 tsp **ground cinnamon**

225 g/8 oz frozen **butternut squash**

225 g/8 oz fresh or frozen **baby carrots**

2 x 400 g/14 oz/large cans of **flageolet beans**, drained and rinsed

150 ml/¼ pt/⅔ cup boiling **vegetable stock**

15 ml/1 tbsp **clear honey**

15 ml/1 tbsp **Thai green curry paste**

Salt and freshly ground black pepper

A little chopped fresh or frozen **parsley**

1   Scrub the eggs in cold water and wrap in greaseproof (waxed) paper, if you prefer. This just makes them less slippery when you peel them.

2   Put the oil, onion, garlic, cinnamon, squash, carrots and flageolet beans in the crock pot.

3   Blend the stock with the honey and curry paste and stir gently into the pot to mix everything together. Add the eggs.

4   Cover and cook on High for 2 hours or Low for 4 hours until everything is tender.

5   Taste and re-season, if necessary. Break up any large pieces of squash.

6   Lift out the eggs, remove the shells (be careful as they'll be hot) and cut into quarters. Spoon the flageolet mixture into warm bowls and top with the egg quarters. Serve sprinkled with chopped parsley.

Cook's tip
• Changing the type of beans and/or squash will alter the finished flavour. Don't be afraid to experiment.

chick pea casserole

4

2 hrs HIGH
or **4** hrs LOW

Warm pitta bread and a mixed salad

450 g/1 lb ready-washed fresh or thawed frozen leaf **spinach**

5 ml/1 tsp **chopped garlic** from a jar, or 1 **garlic clove**, chopped

2 x 400 g/14 oz/large cans of **chick peas** (garbanzos), drained

400 g/14 oz/large can of **chopped tomatoes**

5 ml/1 tsp **ground cinnamon**

2.5 ml/½ tsp **dried oregano**

Salt and freshly ground black pepper

120 ml/4 fl oz/½ cup **crème fraîche**

100 g/4 oz/½ cup crumbled **Feta cheese**

1   If using fresh spinach, put it in the crock pot and squash it with your hands to compact it. If using thawed frozen, squeeze out as much moisture as possible before putting it in the crock pot.

2   Scatter the garlic over the spinach, then add all the remaining ingredients except the crème fraîche and Feta cheese.

3   Cover and cook on High for 2 hours or Low for 4 hours until everything is cooked and full of flavour.

4   Gently stir in the crème fraîche, cover and leave to stand for 5 minutes.

5   Taste and re-season, if necessary. Serve in bowls, sprinkled with the Feta.

6   Accompany with warm pitta bread and a mixed salad.

Cook's tip
• You can add some sliced olives to this dish, if you like them.

baked bean loaf

4-6

2 hrs HIGH
or **4** hrs LOW

Crusty bread
and salad

A little **oil** for greasing

6 rashers (slices) of **rindless streaky bacon**

400 g/14 oz/large can of **baked beans in tomato sauce**

30 ml/2 tbsp **dried onion flakes**

50 g/2 oz/1 cup **dried breadcrumbs**

30 ml/2 tbsp **tomato ketchup** (catsup)

5 ml/1 tsp **yeast extract**

2.5 ml/½ tsp **dried mixed herbs**

2 **eggs**, beaten

Salt and freshly ground black pepper

1   Grease a 450 g/1 lb loaf tin and line with the bacon rashers, side by side widthways across the tin, so the long sides and base are covered and the ends are left unlined.

2   Mix together all the remaining ingredients and turn into the tin. Cover with greased foil, twisting and folding under the rim to secure.

3   Place in the crock pot and pour round enough boiling water to come half-way up the sides of the tin.

4   Cover and cook on High for 2 hours or Low for 4 hours until firm to the touch.

5   Remove from the pot, leave to cool for 10 minutes, then turn out and slice. Alternatively, leave until cold before slicing.

6   Serve warm or cold with crusty bread and salad.

Freezing tip

• Separate slices with greaseproof (waxed) paper, wrap and freeze for up to three months.

black-eyed bean stew

4

2 hrs HIGH
or **4** hrs LOW

Crusty bread

The stew is thrown together in minutes, then left to cook. The cheese takes just a few minutes to grill (broil) when you're ready to serve. If you haven't time, simply omit it altogether or sprinkle the stew with some grated cheese, but I do recommend you try the lovely salty Halloumi slices if you can.

A good handful of **frozen diced onion**, or 1 **fresh onion**, chopped

30 ml/2 tbsp **olive oil**, plus extra for drizzling

2 good handfuls of **frozen grilled (bell) peppers**

2 x 400 g/14 oz/large cans of **black-eyed beans**, drained

150 ml/¼ pt/⅔ cup **passata** (sieved tomatoes)

30 ml/2 tbsp **tomato purée** (paste)

5 ml/1 tsp **chopped garlic** from a jar, or 1 **garlic clove**, chopped

2.5 ml/½ tsp **ground coriander**

Salt and freshly ground black pepper

12 **cherry tomatoes**

15 ml/1 tbsp chopped fresh or frozen **coriander (cilantro)**

250 g/9 oz block **Halloumi cheese**

1   Mix the onion with the olive oil in the crock pot. Stir in all the remaining ingredients except the chopped coriander and the cheese.

2   Cover and cook on High for 2 hours or Low for 4 hours until everything is bathed in a rich sauce.

3   Stir the chopped coriander into the stew.

4   Cut the cheese into eight slices and place on foil on the grill (broiler) rack. Drizzle with olive oil and add a good grinding of pepper. Grill for 2 minutes or until sizzling, then turn over the slices and grill the other sides.

5   Spoon the stew into warm bowls, top with the cheese slices and any oil on the foil.

6   Serve hot with crusty bread.

Serving tip
• The texture of this dish is similar to chilli beans, but without the heat.

vegetable-based dishes

I've used a lot of frozen vegetables in these recipes because they are nutritionally very good and, of course, there is no preparation involved – which is the ethos of this book. In some cases I have given you the choice of fresh or frozen when little or no preparation is necessary for the fresh variety – such as when baby carrots are called for – and, even when I don't, there is nothing to stop you using fresh ingredients and shelling, chopping or trimming and cutting up if you prefer! I had never really used many of these frozen vegetables before writing this book but, I have to say, they've worked really well. I think I shall always keep a packet of frozen diced onion in the freezer for when I can't be bothered to chop or don't want onion fingers!

Tips for great slow-cooked vegetables

- Root vegetables tend to cook quite slowly in the slow cooker so remember that when planning.

- Always put root vegetables at the bottom of the crock pot.

- Frozen vegetables can be cooked from frozen.

- Frozen chopped onions can save loads of time chopping!

- If cooking vegetables from frozen and the pieces are very large, break them up before serving.

- The bags of frozen mixed peppers add plenty of colour as well as flavour without having to buy several fresh ones and only using halves.

- If a recipe calls for 450 g/1 lb of a vegetable and your pack is 500 g, use it all.

bean, squash & barley braise

4-6

2 hrs HIGH
or **4** hrs LOW

Crusty bread
and a crisp
green salad

Chef's note

Pearl barley has become one of my favourite grains, particularly in the slow cooker, because it behaves perfectly. It retains its nutty texture and the grains stay separate even when fully cooked. Here you don't even have to prepare the cheese, just buy a piece and crumble it in.

350 g/12 oz/generous 1⅔ cups **pearl barley**

15 ml/1 tbsp **olive oil**

225 g/8 oz **frozen baby broad (fava) beans**

225 g/8 oz **frozen butternut squash**

30 ml/2 tbsp **dried onion flakes**

2.5 ml/½ tsp **chopped garlic** from a jar, or 1 small **garlic clove**, chopped

900 ml/1½ pts/3¾ cups boiling **vegetable stock**

Salt and freshly ground black pepper

5 ml/1 tsp **dried sage**

150 g/5 oz **Dolcelatte cheese**

90 ml/6 tbsp **single (light) cream**

15 ml/1 tbsp **dried chives**, plus extra to garnish

1   Mix the barley with the oil in the crock pot until all the grains are glistening.

2   Add all the remaining ingredients except the cheese, cream and chives. Stir well.

3   Cover and cook on High for 2 hours or Low for 4 hours until the barley and vegetables are tender.

4   Turn off the slow cooker. Break up any large pieces of squash, then crumble in the cheese and gently stir in the cream and chives. Cover and leave for 5 minutes.

5   Spoon into warm bowls and sprinkle with extra chives.

6   Serve with crusty bread and a crisp green salad to follow.

Cook's tip

• Dolcelatte has a lovely creamy texture, but you could use other blue cheese, as long as it's not too strongly flavoured.

potato & onion baked omelette

4

2 hrs HIGH
or 4 hrs LOW

Salad and pickles

Chef's note

This is a cross between a Spanish omelette and a quiche without the crust! It can be cut into squares and served warm with some warm passata flavoured with garlic or basil or cold with salad and pickles. I would not normally recommend using canned potatoes and have never used canned fried onions before but they do work in this!

550 g/1¼ lb cooked **leftover potatoes** or a large can of **potatoes**, drained

390 g/14 oz/large can of **fried onions**

2.5 ml/½ tsp **dried mixed herbs**

5 **eggs**, beaten

60 ml/4 tbsp **milk**

Salt and freshly ground black pepper

1 Roughly cut up the potatoes and spread out in a shallow rectangular dish that will just fit in a large oval crock pot. Stir in the can of onions and add the herbs.

2 Beat the eggs with the milk and some salt and pepper and pour over.

3 Cover the dish with foil and place in the crock pot. Pour round enough boiling water to come half-way up the sides of the dish.

4 Cover and cook on High for 2 hours or Low for 4 hours until set.

5 Remove from the crock pot and leave to cool for a few minutes before cutting into quarters, if serving warm, or leave until cold before cutting. Serve with salad and pickles.

Cook's tips
- If the canned potatoes are packed in brine, add salt sparingly.
- Experiment and try frozen diced mixed vegetables or sliced peppers instead of potatoes.

garlic mushrooms

4-6

2 hrs HIGH
or **4** hrs LOW

Crusty bread

90 ml/6 tbsp fruity **white wine**

75 ml/5 tbsp boiling **water**

10 ml/2 tsp **chopped garlic** from a jar, or 2 **garlic cloves**, chopped

8–12 large **open mushrooms**, stalks trimmed, if necessary

8–12 tiny knobs of **butter**

Salt and freshly ground black pepper

120 ml/4 fl oz/½ cup **double (heavy) cream**

30 ml/2 tbsp chopped fresh or frozen **parsley**

1   Pour the wine and boiling water into the crock pot and add the garlic. Add the mushrooms in an even layer and top each with a tiny knob of butter. Season well.

2   Cover and cook on High for 2 hours or Low for 4 hours until the mushrooms are really tender with a rich flavour (they can sit for longer, if necessary).

3   Turn up the cooker to High, if on Low. Pour in the cream and add the parsley. Gently stir round, taking care not to break up the mushrooms. Cover and leave to stand for 5 minutes.

4   Transfer the mushrooms to small warm plates. Stir the juices, taste, re-season, if necessary, then spoon over the mushrooms.

5   Serve with crusty bread.

Cook's tip

• Use dry cider instead of wine, if you prefer.

warm asparagus mousse

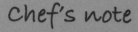

Chef's note

Mousses normally involve separating eggs, fancy folding with a delicate hand and complicated instructions. Not here – just canned asparagus, some eggs and cream, whizzed up together, flavoured with herbs and lightly cooked.

4-6

3 hrs LOW

Wholemeal toast and a mixed salad

---

410 g/14½ oz/large can of **cut asparagus spears**

---

3 **eggs**

---

15 ml/1 tbsp chopped fresh or frozen **parsley**

---

5 ml/1 tsp **dried chives**, plus extra to garnish

---

300 ml/½ pt/1¼ cups **single (light) cream**

A little **butter** or **oil** for greasing

---

120 ml/4 fl oz/½ cup **mayonnaise**

A few drops of **lemon juice**

---

1   Drain the asparagus, reserving the liquid. Tip the asparagus into a blender or food processor and add the eggs, herbs and cream. Blend until smooth, then season to taste.

2   Grease an 18 cm/6 in soufflé dish and pour in the asparagus mixture. Stand the dish in the crock pot and pour round enough boiling water to come half-way up the sides of the dish.

3   Cover and cook on Low for 3 hours until set.

4   Meanwhile, mix the mayonnaise with a little of the reserved asparagus liquid to thin it to pouring consistency. Sharpen with just a few drops of lemon juice and season to taste.

5   Lift the mousse out of the crock pot and sprinkle with a few dried chives.

6   Serve spooned on to plates with a little of the mayonnaise sauce drizzled over, with wholemeal toast and a large mixed salad.

Cook's tip

• You can also make individual ones in six ramekin dishes (custard cups), in which case they'll take only 2 hours to cook. You'll need a large crock pot and may need to rest one or two ramekins on top, balanced on the rims of the other ones, so as not to damage the mousses.

spinach & ricotta lasagne

4

3 hrs LOW

Garlic bread and a mixed salad

Chef's note

Spinach, ricotta and pasta is a well-known combination. Here there is no pre-cooking of the vegetable, no chopping or grating and no complicated sauce. Consequently, it's a version of a classic dish without the classic hassle!

225 g/8 oz **frozen chopped spinach**, thawed

200 g/7 oz/scant 1 cup **Ricotta cheese**

1 large **egg**, beaten

60 ml/4 tbsp grated **Parmesan cheese**

1.5 ml/¼ tsp **ground nutmeg**

15 ml/1 tbsp **milk**

Salt and freshly ground black pepper

8 sheets of **no-need-to-pre-cook green lasagne**

6 **sun-blush tomatoes**, torn into pieces

200 g/7 oz/scant 1 cup **crème fraîche**

10 ml/2 tsp **cornflour** (cornstarch)

10 ml/2 tsp **dried chives**

1   Drain the spinach well through a sieve (strainer) over the sink, pressing it with the back of a spoon to remove all the excess moisture. Place in a bowl and mix with the Ricotta, the egg, half the Parmesan and the nutmeg. Season with a little salt and lots of pepper.

2   Put the milk in a shallow rectangular dish that will just fit in a large crock pot. Top with two sheets of lasagne. Spread a third of the spinach mixture over and scatter with a few bits of sun-blush tomato. Top with two more sheets of pasta. Repeat the layers until the ingredients are used, finishing with a layer of pasta.

3   Beat together the crème fraîche with the remaining Parmesan and the cornflour until smooth. Spoon on top of the lasagne and sprinkle with the chives. Place in the crock pot and pour round enough boiling water to come half-way up the sides of the dish.

4   Cook on Low for 3 hours until the pasta feels tender when a knife is inserted down through the centre.

5   Serve hot with garlic bread and a mixed salad.

Serving tip
• Throw some olives into the salad for a real Italian feel.

Cook's tip
• You can substitute any white soft cheese for Ricotta.

vegetable curry with paneer

4

3 hrs HIGH
or **6** hrs LOW

Rice and chapattis

Chef's note

Paneer is an Indian pressed curd cheese that is readily available in supermarkets. It is also easy to make – but that's for another book! This curry is often served as a side dish without the cheese, but it is a satisfying main dish when served with rice and chapatis or naan breads.

A good handful of **frozen diced onion**, or 1 **fresh onion**, chopped

10 ml/2 tsp softened **butter**

5 ml/1 tsp **chopped garlic** from a jar, or 1 **garlic clove**, chopped

15 ml/1 tbsp mild **curry paste**

15 ml/1 tbsp **garam masala**

175 g/6 oz **creamed coconut**

600 ml/1 pt/2½ cups boiling **water**

30 ml/2 tbsp **tomato purée** (paste)

5 ml/1 tsp **salt**

15 ml/1 tbsp **lime juice**

700 g/1½ lb **frozen casserole vegetables** (chunky ones, not small dice)

12 washed **baby potatoes**

1 **bay leaf**

350 g/12 oz block of **paneer**, diced

1 Mix the onion and butter in the crock pot. Add the garlic, curry paste and garam masala.

2 Blend the creamed coconut with the boiling water and tomato purée until the coconut is melting (it doesn't matter if it's still a bit lumpy). Stir in the salt and lime juice.

3 Put the vegetables and potatoes in the crock pot and pour the sauce over. Add the bay leaf.

4 Cover and cook on High for 3 hours or Low for 6 hours until the vegetables are tender and the sauce is thickened.

5 Discard the bay leaf, taste and re-season, if necessary. Gently fold in the paneer. Cover and leave to stand for 5 minutes.

6 Serve in bowls with rice and chapattis.

Serving tip

- This is also good served topped with poached eggs (how often do I say that?).

couscous-stuffed peppers

4

3 hrs HIGH
or **6** hrs LOW

Crusty bread
and salad

Chef's note

You have to prepare the peppers for this dish, but cutting off the tops and pulling out the core and seeds is hardly exhausting or skilful! It makes a quick-to-prepare, easy lunch or supper dish that can be served hot or cold with some crusty bread and salad.

4 large (bell) **peppers**

400 g/14 oz/large can of **ratatouille**

50 g/2 oz/$\frac{1}{3}$ cup **couscous**

2.5 ml/$\frac{1}{2}$ tsp **dried oregano**

100 g/4 oz/1 cup grated strong **Cheddar cheese**

Salt and freshly ground black pepper

450 ml/$\frac{3}{4}$ pt/2 cups boiling **vegetable** or **chicken stock**

1   Carefully cut the tops off the peppers about 8 mm/⅓ in down from the stalk end and retain. Pull out the cores and seeds. Tap the peppers firmly on the work surface, cut-sides down, to remove any loose seeds. Make sure the peppers will stand upright; if not, trim a very thin slice off the bases (take care not to make a hole in the flesh, though).

2   Mix the ratatouille with the couscous, oregano and 50 g/2 oz/ ½ cup of the cheese. Taste and add a little salt and pepper, if necessary.

3   Stand the peppers in the crock pot and spoon the ratatouille mixture into them. Top with the remaining cheese and rest the pepper 'lids' on top. Pour the boiling stock around.

4   Cover and cook on High for 3 hours or Low for 6 hours until the peppers are tender.

5   Transfer the peppers to plates and spoon a little of the cooking stock over, if liked. Alternatively, leave to cool, then chill before serving.

6   Serve with crusty bread and salad.

Cook's tip

• I use red or yellow peppers because they keep their lovely bright colour, but any colour will work fine in this dish.

spinach & peanut loaf

4

3 hrs HIGH
or 6 hrs LOW

Jacket potatoes,
grated cheese
and sweetcorn

Chef's note

This is another delicious vegetable loaf that is simplicity itself. Using a stuffing mix adds the right texture and flavour without any effort. It's really good served hot, but can also be left until cold and served sliced with salad and pickled beetroot (red beet).

225 g/8 oz **frozen leaf spinach**, thawed

75 g/3 oz **sage, onion and lemon (or garlic) stuffing mix**

5 ml/1 tsp **chopped garlic** from a jar, or 1 **garlic clove**, chopped

75 g/3 oz/¾ cup **roasted peanuts**

Salt and freshly ground black pepper

45 ml/3 heaped tbsp **peanut butter**

120 ml/4 fl oz/½ cup boiling **water**

1 **egg**

5 ml/1 tsp **yeast extract**

A little **sunflower oil** for greasing

450 ml/¾ pt/2 cups **passata** (sieved tomatoes) with onion

1 Squeeze out the spinach to remove as much moisture as possible. Place in a mixing bowl.

2 Add the stuffing mix, garlic, peanuts and some salt and pepper. Blend the peanut butter with the boiling water and stir in. Beat the egg with the yeast extract and add. Mix until everything is thoroughly blended.

3 Turn into a greased 450 g/1 lb loaf tin (pan) and cover with foil, twisting and folding under the rim to secure. Place in the crock pot and pour round enough boiling water to come half-way up the sides of the tin.

4 Cover and cook on High for 2–3 hours or Low for 4–6 hours until firm.

5 Leave the loaf to cool for 3–4 minutes. Meanwhile, heat the passata in a saucepan. Turn out the loaf on to a warm serving dish.

6 Serve the loaf sliced with the warm passata, jacket potatoes topped with grated cheese, and sweetcorn.

Cook's tip
• If you have one, use a microwave to bake the potatoes.

cauliflower cheese

4 hrs HIGH
or 8 hrs LOW

Crusty bread

Chef's note

This is simplicity itself! You put the still-frozen veg in the pot, mix a few other ingredients together, spoon over and leave to cook. It's delicious on its own with crusty bread or try it with bacon, chops, fish or chicken.

700 g/1½ lb **frozen cauliflower florets**

30 ml/2 tbsp **cornflour** (cornstarch)

Salt and freshly ground black pepper

400 g/14 oz/1 large can of **chopped tomatoes**

100 g/4 oz/1 cup grated **Cheddar cheese**

200 ml/7 fl oz/scant 1 cup **crème fraîche**

2 good handfuls of **cornflakes**

1   Put the florets in the crock pot and sprinkle the cornflour
    over. Mix it together thoroughly with your hands. Make sure
    there isn't lots of cornflour in the corners of the pot. Season
    well and add the tomatoes.

2   Mix about 75 g/3 oz/¾ cup of the Cheddar with the crème
    fraîche. Spoon over and spread out the mixture fairly evenly
    (it won't cover the vegetables completely).

3   Scatter the remaining cheese on top, then crush the
    cornflakes over.

4   Cover and cook on High for 2–3 hours or Low for 6–8 hours
    (depending on the size of the florets) until the vegetables are
    cooked to your liking and the cheese has melted. Check after
    the shorter time if you like some 'bite' in your vegetables.

5   Serve straight from the pot with crusty bread.

Cook's tip

• This dish is good made with a mixture of broccoli and
  cauliflower, too.

sweet & hot peppers & eggs

4

3 hrs HIGH or 6 hrs LOW

Crusty bread

Chef's note

You can prepare your own peppers by cutting off the tops, pulling out the seeds and then slicing them but, for total convenience, I'm suggesting using frozen. The choice is yours, though. If you like perfect soft-cooked eggs, poach them conventionally instead of putting them in the slow cooker.

60 ml/4 tbsp **olive oil**

A good handful of **frozen diced onion**, or 1 **fresh onion**, chopped

4 good handfuls of **frozen sliced mixed (bell) peppers**, or 4 small different-coloured fresh **peppers**, sliced

½ x 200 g/7 oz jar of red or green **pickled sliced jalapeño peppers**

2 x 400 g/14 oz/large cans of **chopped tomatoes**

5 ml/1 tsp **caster (superfine) sugar**

Salt and freshly ground black pepper

100 g/4 oz/1 cup **frozen peas**, thawed (optional)

4 **eggs**

1   Mix together all the ingredients except the peas, if using, and eggs in the crock pot.

2   Cover and cook on High for 2–3 hours or Low for 4–6 hours until the vegetables are tender.

3   Add the peas, if using. Taste and re-season, if necessary. Turn down the slow cooker to Low.

4   Make four wells in the mixture and break an egg into each. Cover and cook for 10–15 minutes until the eggs are cooked to your liking.

5   Serve straight away with crusty bread.

Cook's tips

- If preparing the peppers from scratch, rinse them under running water to wash away the seeds.
- You could add sweetcorn instead of peas.

mushrooms in wine with feta

4

3 hrs HIGH
or **6** hrs LOW

Rice

Here mushrooms are gently cooked in white wine and tomatoes with garlic, oregano and bay leaves, then served topped with crumbled Feta cheese on a bed of rice.

30 ml/2 tbsp **olive oil**

30 ml/2 tbsp **dried onion flakes**

150 ml/¼ pt/⅔ cup dry **white wine**

2 **bay leaves**

2.5 ml/½ tsp **dried oregano**

5 ml/1 tsp **chopped garlic** from a jar (or 1 **garlic clove**, chopped)

450 g/1 lb small **button mushrooms**

400 g/14 oz/1 large can of **chopped tomatoes**

Salt and freshly ground black pepper

100 g/4 oz/½ cup **Feta cheese**, crumbled

15 ml/1 tbsp chopped fresh or frozen **parsley**

1   Mix everything except the salt and pepper, cheese and parsley in the crock pot. Season well.

2   Cover and cook on High for 2–3 hours or Low for 4–6 hours. Taste and re-season if necessary and discard the bay leaves.

3   Spoon over rice in bowls and garnish with the crumbled Feta cheese and parsley.

4   Serve with boiled rice.

Cook's tip

• To make this dish more substantial, try adding a large can of drained chick peas (garbanzos) at the start of cooking.

rocket & goats' cheese tart

4

2 hrs HIGH
or 4 hrs LOW

Complete meal
in itself

1 ready-baked **pastry case** (pie shell)

50 g/2 oz packet of **rocket leaves** (arugula)

225 g/8 oz/small can of **chopped tomatoes**

120 g/4½ oz cylinder of **goats' cheese**, cut into six slices

50 g/2 oz/very small can of **anchovies**, drained

2.5 ml/½ tsp **dried basil**

Freshly ground black pepper

1   Put the pastry case, still in its foil container, in the crock pot. Add the rocket and squeeze gently to crush it slightly.

2   Spread the tomatoes over the rocket, then arrange the slices of cheese on top. Arrange the anchovies over in a lattice pattern and sprinkle with the basil. Season with some pepper.

3   Cover and cook on High for 2 hours or Low for 4 hours until the rocket is wilted and the cheese soft and melting.

4   Serve warm.

Serving tip

- There are some very strong flavours in this tart, so it doesn't need any accompaniment.

grilled pepper tart

4

2 hrs HIGH
or 4 hrs LOW

A green salad

Chef's note

I love making these quick tarts in the slow cooker – and this one is even simpler than the others in the book! I like this one served warm, but it is equally good served cold for a packed lunch or as part of a buffet.

45 ml/3 tbsp **tomato purée** (paste)

1 ready-baked **pastry case** (pie shell)

5 ml/1 tsp **dried basil**

4 good handfuls of **frozen grilled (bell) peppers**

Salt and freshly ground black pepper

A good handful of ready-grated **Cheddar cheese**

12 slices of stoned (pitted) green or black **olives** (optional)

1   Spread the tomato purée in the pastry case, still in its foil container, and sprinkle with the basil. Place in the crock pot.

2   Spread out the peppers in the case and season with a little salt and lots of pepper.

3   Sprinkle with the Cheddar and arrange the olive slices on top, if using.

4   Cover and cook on High for 2 hours or Low for 4 hours until the peppers are soft and the cheese melted.

5   Serve warm or cold with a green salad.

Cook's tip
- Try it with crumbled blue cheese instead of Cheddar.

fruit-based dishes & other desserts

This book is mostly about main courses because that's what you need every day and what takes most time to prepare. However, I felt there was a place for just a few quick and easy-to-make desserts that cook so well in the slow cooker. If you're making a salad for a main course, for instance, it's good to have something tasty for pudding simmering in the pot! Some, though, are best left to cool then chilled before serving – wonderful to bring out of the fridge with a flourish!

Tips for great slow-cooked desserts

- You can make delicious fruit compôte without added sugar that makes a great dessert. Just use the dried fruits you have to hand and adapt the recipe on page 238.

- The slow cooker can be very useful for making a delicious dessert for guests, such as creamy rice pudding. You can concentrate on the main course and leave the dessert to cook away quietly.

- Whole fruits poach beautifully in the slow cooker.

- You can stew fruits in the slow cooker to serve on their own or use to fill pies or crumbles.

creamy rice pudding

Chef's note

Rice pudding is perfect when cooked in the slow cooker. The result is always creamy, soft and tender – particularly when you use canned evaporated milk – and there's no brown skin either!

75 g/3 oz/⅓ cup **round-grain (pudding) rice**

50 g/2 oz/¼ cup **caster (superfine) sugar**

410 g/14½ oz/large can of **evaporated milk**

5 ml/1 tsp **natural vanilla essence** (extract)

1   Put the rice in the crock pot and sprinkle the sugar over. Pour in the can of evaporated milk, then fill the empty can with water and tip into the pot as well. Half-fill it again and add.

2   Add the vanilla essence and stir everything together thoroughly.

3   Cover and cook on High for 3 hours or Low for 6 hours until thick, creamy and the rice is tender.

4   Stir gently, then serve hot or cold.

Cook's tip

• Try sprinkling in a couple of handfuls of raisins, sultanas (golden raisins) or chopped dried apricots before adding the milk for a lovely, fruity pudding.

mulled winter fruit salad

4

2 hrs HIGH or **4** hrs LOW

Thick cream or Greek-style yoghurt

250 g/9 oz packet of **dried fruit salad**

450 ml/¾ pt/2 cups **apple juice**

1 piece of **cinnamon stick**

2 **whole cloves**

1 **star anise**

1   Put all the ingredients in the crock pot.

2   Cover and cook on High for 2 hours or Low for 4 hours until tender and bathed in syrup.

3   Discard the spices.

4   Serve hot or cold with thick cream or Greek-style yoghurt.

Cook's tip

• I've used separate spices, but you could use a mulled wine sachet instead.

hot raspberry fool

4

2 hrs LOW

Shortbread fingers

Chef's note

This dessert is an ingenious way of making a fruit fool without all the stirring that is essential when you cook one conventionally. This custard cooks so slowly it doesn't form lumps and the whole thing is simply served straight from the individual dishes.

30 ml/2 tbsp **cornflour** (cornstarch)

200 ml/7 fl oz/scant 1 cup **milk**

1 **egg**

60 ml/4 tbsp **caster (superfine) sugar**

5 ml/1 tsp natural **vanilla essence** (extract)

200 ml/7 fl oz/scant 1 cup **single (light) cream**

100 g/4 oz ripe **raspberries**

1   Blend the cornflour with 60 ml/4 tbsp of the milk in a bowl. Whisk in the egg, sugar and vanilla. Whisk in the remaining milk and the cream.

2   Reserve four raspberries for decoration and divide the remainder between four ramekins (custard cups). Pour the custard mixture over.

3   Stand the dishes in the crock pot and pour round enough boiling water to come half-way up the sides of the ramekins. Cover and cook on Low for 2 hours until set.

4   Decorate with the reserved raspberries and serve with shortbread fingers.

Cook's tip
• Try it with other berries, such as blueberries, blackberries or sliced strawberries.

peaches in kirsch & wine

6

3 hrs LOW

Thin almond biscuits or ratafias

600 ml/1 pint/2½ cups dry **white wine**

175 g/6 oz/¾ cup **caster (superfine) sugar**

60 ml/4 tbsp **kirsch**

6 large, ripe **peaches**

1 piece of **cinnamon stick**

2 handfuls of whole **blanched almonds**

Chef's note

Whole peaches are gently poached in a wine syrup with a dash of kirsch to give it a kick. The slow cooker cooks them to perfection without them losing their shape and there is no need to peel them either.

1   Mix the wine with the sugar and kirsch in the crock pot. Stir until the sugar has dissolved.

2   Add the peaches, cinnamon stick and almonds.

3   Cover and cook on Low for 2–3 hours until the fruit is tender. Discard the cinnamon stick.

4   Serve warm, or cool then chill before serving with thin almond biscuits or ratafias.

Cook's tip

• You can also try using nectarines or plums in place of the peaches.

rhubarb in ginger wine

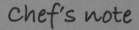

Chef's note

Rhubarb and ginger has always been a great flavour combination. Here I've simply cut up some sticks of rhubarb, popped them in the crock pot with some sugar, water and a good splash of ginger wine and left them to cook.

4

4 hrs LOW

Custard or cream and shortbread fingers

450 g/1 lb **rhubarb**

50 g/2 oz/¼ cup **caster (superfine) sugar**

90 ml/6 tbsp boiling **water**

60 ml/4 tbsp **ginger wine**

1   Trim the rhubarb, cut it into short lengths and spread out in the crock pot.

2   Sprinkle the sugar over, then add the water and ginger wine.

3   Cover and cook on Low for 4 hours until tender but still holding its shape.

4   Serve hot or cold with custard or cream and shortbread fingers.

Cook's tip

• For extra zing, add 5 ml/1 tsp of finely chopped root ginger from a jar.

smooth coffee pudding

6-8

2 hrs LOW

250 ml/8 fl oz/1 cup boiling **water**

15 ml/3 heaped tsp **instant coffee granules**

100 g/4 oz/½ cup **caster (superfine) sugar**

6 **eggs**

300 ml/½ pint/1¼ cups **extra-thick cream**

For the fondant:

45 ml/3 heaped tbsp good-quality **chocolate spread**

45 ml/3 tbsp **milk**

Chef's note

This smooth, velvety dessert sets in the crock pot and is then cooled and decorated with extra-thick cream. You can use whipped, if you prefer, but that's more work! A gloriously rich chocolate sauce is then trickled over – delicious!

1   Mix the boiling water with the coffee and sugar until dissolved. Whisk in the eggs and strain into a 15 cm/6 in soufflé dish.

2   Stand the dish in the crock pot and pour round enough boiling water to come half-way up the side of the dish.

3   Cover and cook on Low for 2 hours until set.

4   Remove from the crock pot and leave to cool, then chill.

5   To make the fondant, blend the chocolate spread with the milk to form a thick pouring consistency.

6   When ready to serve, pile the cream on top of the pudding. Using a small spoon, trickle a little of the chocolate fondant over the cream. Serve the rest in a small jug.

Cook's tip

• Even the sauce is not exactly an effort – but to cheat even more you could use bought chocolate sauce.

chocolate & chestnut torte

8-10

5 hrs LOW

I had already designed a version of this for the slow cooker but never with chocolate spread! It's an outrageous cheat, but the result is just as good as if you've slaved over it for hours! You don't even have to grate any chocolate for the coating!

For the torte:

A little **oil** for greasing

400 g/14 oz jar of **chocolate spread** (plain, not with hazelnuts (filberts))

45 ml/3 tbsp **cocoa (unsweetened chocolate) powder**

75 g /3 oz/⅓ cup softened **butter**

435 g/15½ oz/large can of **unsweetened chestnut purée** (paste)

50 g/2 oz/¼ cup **caster (superfine) sugar**

4 **eggs**

5 ml/1 tsp natural **vanilla essence** (extract)

For the coating:

100 g/4 oz/1 cup **plain (semi-sweet) chocolate chips**

120 ml/4 fl oz/½ cup **double (heavy) cream**

30 ml/2 tbsp **icing (confectioners') sugar**

1   To make the torte, grease a 20 cm/8 in springform cake tin and line the base with baking parchment. Stand the tin on a sheet of foil and press it up the outside of the tin (to protect the cake from the water).

2   Beat together all the torte ingredients in a bowl until thoroughly blended, then tip into the prepared tin. Cover the tin with foil, twisting and folding under the rim to secure.

3   Pour about 5 mm/¼ in of boiling water into the crock pot to cover the base and stand the tin in the pot.

4   Cook on Low for 4–5 hours until fairly firm.

5   Remove from the crock pot and leave to cool in the tin.

6   To make the coating, put the chocolate chips in a saucepan with the icing sugar and the cream. Heat gently, stirring all the time with a wooden spoon, until thick. Leave to cool slightly until it has a thick, coating consistency.

7   Remove the torte from the tin and place on a plate. Spoon the coating over, spreading it out with a palette knife so it coats the top and sides of the torte completely. Wipe the edge of the plate, if necessary, to clean up any excess chocolate.

8   Leave to set. You can chill it until the next day if not serving straight away, but the coating will become a little less shiny.

Freezing tip
• This superb torte can be frozen, too, so it's great if you are entertaining and want to make it in advance.

lemon tart

I know you can buy
ready-made lemon tarts,
but this one tastes so
good and you can claim
you made it – even
though you didn't have to
grate, squeeze or roll out!
What's more, unlike when
you bake it in the oven,
there is no chance of it
overbrowning on top or
drying out.

6

3 hrs
LOW

1 ready-baked **sweet pastry case** (pie shell)

350 g/12 oz jar of **lemon curd**

15 ml/1 tbsp bottled **lemon juice**

1 **egg**

Icing (confectioners') sugar for dusting

1 Put the pastry case, still in its foil container, in the crock pot. Beat together the lemon curd, lemon juice and egg, and spoon into the case.

2 Cover and cook on Low for 2–3 hours until set.

3 Carefully remove from the crock pot and leave to cool, then chill.

4 Dust with icing sugar before serving.

Cook's tip
• Try it with orange or lime curd, too.

custard tart

Chef's note

This is a nursery favourite that can be quite complicated when cooked conventionally. Here I've cheated mercilessly but the result is a very good custard tart, lightly dusted with nutmeg, that, once cooked, wobbles and shimmers in its pastry case in a lusciously tempting way.

1 ready-baked **sweet pastry case** (pie shell)

2 **eggs**

100 ml/3½ fl oz/scant ½ cup **milk**

425 g/15 oz/large can of **ready-made custard**

25 g/1 oz/2 tbsp **caster (superfine) sugar**

A little **ground nutmeg**

1   Put the pastry case, still in its foil container, in the crock pot.

2   Beat the eggs with the milk, then beat in the custard and sugar.

3   Pour into the pastry case and dust with a little nutmeg. Cover and bake on Low for 3 hours until just set.

4   Carefully remove from the slow cooker and leave to cool until warm, or cool completely then chill before serving.

Serving tip

• Add a splash of colour by serving with a spoonful of mixed summer berries – bought ready-prepared, of course!

Cook's tip

• You can cook the custard mixture in a dish with enough water to come half-way up the side as a simple baked custard.

index